The
Beagle
Handbook

Dan Rice, D.V.M.

With Full-color Photos and
Illustrations by Pam Tanzey

BARRON'S

About the Author

Dan Rice, a veterinarian from Colorado, continues to pursue a lifelong writing avocation. A professional member of Dog Writers Association of America, he has written *Waggin' Tails,* an anthology of veterinary practice experiences, as well as a few children's books. *The Beagle Handbook* is the eleventh book he has written for Barron's. His other titles include: *Bengal Cats, Complete Book of Dog Breeding, Complete Book of Cat Breeding, Akitas, Dogs from A to Z (A Dictionary of Canine Terms), The Well Mannered Cat, Brittany, Chesapeake Bay Retrievers, Training Your German Shepherd,* and *The Dog Handbook.* Now retired to sunny Arizona with his wife Marilyn, he manages to stay abreast of pet research and fancy through study and writing.

Cover Photos

Front and back: Isabelle Francais and Chris Sibley; Inside front: Pets by Paulette; Inside back: Isabelle Francais.

Dedication

It's been a habit to dedicate each book of mine to some person or persons who significantly influenced its writing. In keeping with that practice, this book is dedicated to Kris Kraeuter and the great beagling community of America. Beagles may not be the most popular breed in this country, they may not be the dogs for everyone, but those who breed, raise, train, and show this wonderful breed are probably the most cooperative and informative group of people with whom it has been my good fortune to work.

Photo Credits

Norvia Behling: pages viii, 8, 21, 47, 48, 49, 57, 58, 61, 66, 83, 84, 86, 87, 89, 91, 96, 115, 154, 156, 175, 179, 180 top, 180 bottom, 182; Isabelle Francais: pages x, 19, 24, 34, 37, 43, 59, 62, 68, 75, 81, 99, 113, 130, 139, 142, 145, 148, 151, 159, 160, 163, 165, 167, 170, 186; Judith Strom: pages 5, 11, 17, 70, 72, 74, 90, 95, 102, 104, 117, 121, 125, 134, 137; Tara Darling: pages 9, 123, 128, 177; Pets By Paulette: page 14; Susan Green: pages 26, 28, 31, 40, 52, 56, 60, 93, 110, 173, 183; Bonnie Nance: pages 10, 39; Zig Leszczynski: pages 78, 107.

© Copyright 2000 by Barron's Educational Series, Inc.

All inquiries should be addressed to:
Barron's Educational Series, Inc.
250 Wireless Boulevard
Hauppauge, New York 11788
http://www.barronseduc.com

International Standard Book No. 0-7641-1464-6

Library of Congress Catalog Card No. 99-59692

Library of Congress Cataloging-in-Publication Data
Rice, Dan, 1933–
        The beagle handbook / Dan Rice ; illustrations by
Pam Tanzey.
        p.   cm.
        Includes bibliographical references (p.) and index.
        ISBN 0-7641-1464-6 (alk. paper)
        1. Beagle (Dog breed). I. Title.
SF429.B3 R53   2000
636.753'7—dc21   99-59692

Printed in Hong Kong

9 8 7 6 5 4 3 2 1

Important Note

This pet handbook gives advice to the reader about buying and caring for a new dog. The author and the publisher consider it important to point out that the advice given in the book applies to normally developed puppies or adult dogs, obtained from recognized dog breeders or adoption shelters, dogs that have been examined and are in excellent health with good temperament.

Anyone who adopts a grown dog should be aware that the animal has already formed its basic knowledge of human beings and their customs. The new owner should watch the animal carefully, especially its attitude and behavior toward humans. If possible, the new owner should meet the former owners before adopting the dog. If the dog comes from a shelter, the new owner should make an effort to obtain information about the dog's background, personality, and peculiarities. Dogs that come from abusive homes or from homes in which they have been treated abnormally may react to handling in an unnatural manner, and may have a tendency to snap or bite. Dogs with this nature should only be adopted by people who have had experience with such dogs.

Caution is further advised in the association of children with dogs, both puppies and adults, and in meeting other dogs, whether on or off lead.

Well-behaved and carefully supervised dogs may cause damage to someone else's property or cause accidents. It is therefore in the owner's interest to be adequately insured against such eventualities, and we strongly urge all dog owners to purchase a liability policy that covers their dog.

Contents

Preface

Buying a hound puppy is the beginning of a 12- to 15-year commitment. That's a long time to spend with a close companion who has an attitude problem. Wise individuals make an effort to build relationships with human friends whose personalities complement their own. Likewise, prospective dog owners should choose pets whose characters blend with their own. You need voluminous, reliable information about the dog you choose, and if you're thinking Beagle, this book is a great place to start.

Canine housemates should be family members, comrades with whom you can enjoy your leisure hours. Folks who lead quiet lives should choose gentle dogs. Rambunctious, strong-willed dogs work best in homes of dominant, assertive owners.

An easy dog to care for, the Beagle is a companion that demands little and gives tons of affection in return. Beagles are contagiously happy little hounds, always ready for a romp, a walk, or a quiet, affectionate few minutes of your time.

Who can resist a Beagle?

Purchasing a Beagle is only the beginning. Ownership includes more than providing doggy necessities and allowing this merry pet to occupy a cleanable portion of your home. Ownership means building a human-canine relationship that teaches your pet to respect human rules of comportment; at the same time, you must learn and respect your dog's idiosyncrasies.

Your Beagle will communicate with you and give as much love and obedience as you ask for, but affection and communication must be reciprocal. You must understand your Beagle's personality, as well as your role in helping to mold that personality to fit your lifestyle. You will appreciate and enjoy Beagle ownership only after you learn what the Beagle needs and what brings him or her happiness.

This book is designed to give you abundant information about your new Beagle, whether acquired as a puppy or an adult. It offers suggestions to make Beagle ownership a pleasant and rewarding experience.

A history of the canine species and its domestication is presented so you may better understand why

A happy, healthy Beagle pup.

your Beagle's personality and actions are sometimes governed by instinct.

Advice is given to make shopping for your Beagle easier. The puppy selection process, getting acquainted, bonding, and housebreaking techniques are covered.

The latest information is presented relative to Beagle personality, behavioral adjustment, schooling, and hunting. Also included is information about obedience, Canine Good Citizen (CGC) certification, scent games, tracking, agility, conformation showing, and field trials.

A comprehensive discussion of Beagle nutrition is included, with advice on diet, treats, and dangerous foods.

Health, first aid, and emergency procedures, including CPR, are covered. Preventive medicine, Beagle hereditary conditions, the importance of vaccinations, spaying, and castration are included.

Before you buy this book, browse through it. Pick a beagling subject you wish to know more about and, using the index, turn to that page. If I've done my job, you'll find the answer to your query.

Acknowledgments

A labor of love, my work on *The Beagle Handbook* was made easier by many interested people. I owe many thanks to Grace Freedson, Managing Editor of Barron's, for allowing me to undertake this book, and Mark Miele, my Barron's editor, who provided expert guidance. Kris and Jack Kraeuter contributed more than their share, including a wealth of practical information about Beagles, as well as stories and insights into the breed. Kris proved to be a great beagling mentor and evaluated the manuscript, making various suggestions and comments that improved the book. Other beaglers to whom I owe a personal note of gratitude include:
Lee Cord & Cliff Veth (Londonderry MC's Beagles),
Joyce Dayton (Blackhawk Beagles),
James, Sharon, and Trisha Maddex (Ladmar Beagles),
Kerry Schultz (Terwillegar Beagles),
Pat Moscaritolo (Frantricia Beagles),
Rose and Larry Arnold (Rose Run Beagles),
Kathy Forbes (Skyline Beagles),
James R. Frazier, D.V.M. (Someday Beagles),
Ruth Darlene Stewart (Aladar Beagles),
Denise Nord (Chaos Beagles),
Ann H. Roth (Harnett Hounds)

Chapter One

In the Beginning

Evolution of the Dog

If fossil evidence is accepted, your Beagle has roots in a five-toed, weasel-like, tree-climbing animal called *Miacis,* which lived 40 million years ago in the Eocene epoch. According to evolutionary theory, cats, raccoons, bears, hyenas, foxes, wolves, jackals, and dogs share this common progenitor.

Next in the canine evolutionary line was *Cynodictis,* which lived in the Oligocene period about 20 million years ago, followed by *Tomarctus,* some 10 million years ago. *Tomarctus* is reputed to be the direct ancestor of the canine family.

According to evolutionary theory, members of the genus *Canis*, which includes the dog and wolf among others, developed into their present form about a million years ago during the Pleistocene period.

Wolves' Relationship with Humans

Evolutionary speculation places the first domestic dog with man 15,000 years ago. Credible Greek writings mention hunting dog use in about 1300 B.C.

Wild canines survived by hunting, killing, and eating their prey, or by scavenging on prey killed by humans and other predators. It's possible the opposite is true and humans followed and scavenged from wild dog packs' kills. Wild canines had great speed, strength, and endurance, and

Miacis— ancestor of the Beagle.

1

Wolves are more recent canine progenitors.

humans had superior brainpower. The two species eventually compromised instead of competing.

Domestication

It's logical to assume that early in their relationship, human intelligence and abstract thinking gave the human dominance in communal life. Canine survival in human packs depended on dogs' inferior role as followers.

Ancient humans domesticated dogs to assist in herding and hunting.

Domestication probably began when a wolf puppy was taken from its den at an early age, fed, and kept by a human. The more manageable or trainable wolves formed the gene pool used to propagate this captive species, and eventually dogs were molded from a feral species.

Dogs were used as food, for hunting, as draft animals, for guarding, and for herding other animals. Their instinct to kill and eat their charges was suppressed by selective breeding.

Selective Breeding

The dog's physical appearance (phenotype) is quite malleable, and many visible characteristics of dogs that aren't displayed in wolves could have been fixed by selective breeding of their wolf ancestors. Dogs' eyes are generally rounder than those of wolves, who have slitlike eye apertures. Wolf puppies have wider, rounder eyes than their parents. The dog's eyelid anatomy, therefore, could be associated with selection of parents who retain puppylike features into adulthood (neoteny). Similarly, dogs' pendulant ears and shorter muzzles might also be the result of selective breeding and neoteny.

Instinct

This term means an inborn tendency to behave in a way that is characteristic of a species—a natural and unlearned response to a stimulus. Dogs retain certain instincts of their forebears and routinely display these behaviors.

Pack Action

Dog pack instinct is often considered only when discussing dominance. This canine characteristic surfaces in hunting dogs such as the Beagle where cooperation between pack dogs is quite important.

Body Language

Postural display is another canine instinctive characteristic. When meeting a stranger, a dog may raise its back hair (hackles) as a sign of anxiety. The intention is to intimidate the enemy by making the dog look bigger than its opponent.

Tail carriage is an equally important display. For instance, a frightened dog will tuck its tail between the hind legs.

Crouching in subjugation or rolling over on its back represents an instinctive submissive action of an inferior dog.

Placing its forelegs on the ground and lowering the forequarters is an invitation to play and is seen in young wolves as well as domestic canines. When coupled with a wagging tail, it is a display of friendliness.

Olfactory Sense

Turning in circles before lying down is an instinct seen in many dogs. Experts note that because the dogs usually have their noses to the ground when circling, this habit may be associated with seeking the scent of enemies.

Sniffing the wind for the scent trail of another animal is an instinct deeply ingrained in many dogs, especially the Beagle. Scenting ability undoubtedly has been the goal of years of selective breeding, but its origin is instinctive.

Experience

Instincts are hereditary, and they certainly influence dog behavior, but instinct alone can't explain total canine conduct. Neither is behavior the sum of instincts plus conditioning. It includes experience as well.

In his 1895 book *Fetch and Carry*, B. Waters wrote, "The common belief seems to be that the dog acts from the impulse of *instinct* throughout its life. Many people concede no higher mentality to the dog than what comes from instinct, . . . that . . . are independent of experience; while the *dog's knowledge is dependent on experience and education. . . .*"

Experience educates dogs. Dogs watch other animals and mimic their actions. They have the capacity to think, reason, and plan. Blessed with problem-solving ability, the modern dog is a cunning and intelligent animal with a complex mind.

Canine Cognizance

Scent hounds use their scenting endowment, memories, and reasoning abilities to solve retrieving and tracking problems. They scent blood, deduce through experience that a wounded animal or bird must be retrieved first, then reason that they must circle or quarter in the hunting field to find the injured game.

Loyalty, a Noninstinctive Trait

Loyalty seems to go beyond canine instinct. Dogs have proven this quality by forfeiting their lives to defend their owners, by pulling a drowning child from a swimming pool, or by warning sleeping owners of a fire. None of these actions are taught, yet the canine mind somehow reasons and thinks out the problem, then plans and initiates an appropriate action.

Dogs in Literature

One of the earliest historians to include dogs in literature was Homer, the Greek author of *The Odyssey*, in the ninth century B.C. According to Homer, Cerberus, a horrible three-headed dog, guarded the entrance to the underworld.

In 1494 a Greek agricultural instructor, Petrus de Crescentis, documented many lasting tenets referring to dogs in his book, *Field and Furrow Cultivation*. He wrote, "Our daily needs lays it upon us that we must first have good [dog] trackers that they may hunt up the wolves and track them . . . and they must train them with patience."

Dogs appear in every size, shape, and color.

Beagles are experts at tracking.

Thus, Beagle fundamentals were set forth in the fifteenth century. Scenting was emphasized, and the operative word for training was "patience."

Specialization

Specialization followed close on the heels of domestication. Dogs with strong instinctive olfactory abilities were developed to locate game by its scent. Early gene pools for scenthounds included dogs of all sizes and colors. From this pool, trailing breeds of every description were developed. Large scenthounds were used to locate and sometimes kill mountain lions, and smaller hounds became efficient in locating hares, squirrels, and other small game.

Breeds

Breed is defined in *Webster's New World Dictionary* as a "group of animals descended from common ancestors and having similar characteristics, especially when cultivated by humans."

Dog breeds have been specially developed to perform various duties over the course of domestic canine history. However, breed pedigrees weren't methodically compiled until the nineteenth century, with the establishment of the first kennel clubs.

Today's breeds represent standardization of desirable traits, especially those features that have proved useful in the breeds' activities. In breeds like the Beagle, scenting propensity prevails in all members of

Millions of unwanted dogs are destroyed each year.

the breed. Opinions differ among breeders when asked about the relative importance of conformation and proof of hunting ability. However, nearly all beaglers admit that packing mentality, hunting skills, and endurance linger in every member of the breed.

Stewardship

For centuries we've treasured our dogs as living instruments that make our lives more enjoyable and productive. It wasn't always so; in the past, dogs were luxuries only afforded by the affluent. Only wealthy landlords could afford to keep packs of hunting hounds; exclusive hunt clubs alone could maintain a kennel of bird dogs; and royalty bred and ran coursing hounds.

Dogs were safer, if less plentiful, in those bygone days. Overbreeding wasn't a problem, and dog rescue organizations were nonexistent. Dog abuse was rare, and canine husbandry was carefully practiced. Then came the spread of human affluence and with it the desire to own and breed dogs. Backyards overflowed with dogs of every breed, their value was depreciated, and dog overpopulation embraced enormous numbers. Every breed is now represented in shelters and pounds, and millions of unwanted dogs are mercifully destroyed every year.

Such treatment of our faithful companions is undeserved. Dogs' uses have increased as more is discovered about their brainpower; dogs are trained in virtually every field of human assistance. Hearing dogs are popular, dogs are kept by nursing facilities for residents to love and pet, and others are specially trained to help stroke victims, the elderly, and the infirm. Although dogs' true value has increased over the past century, their perceived value has sunk to the level of paper cups. Dogs are often purchased on whims and dumped when no longer wanted. What a shame!

Chapter Two
Birth of the Beagle

Ancestors and Country of Origin

Facts surrounding the Beagle's place of origin are sketchy at best. Most contemporary sources agree that European hounds were developed as a specific type very early in the history of canine domestication. Those early hunting dogs were further divided into gazehounds or coursing dogs, which were guided to their quarry by sight, and scenthounds that perfected the gift of following their prey's track.

Scenthounds were defined further by size; the larger, used to trail stags and other big game, were called Buck Hounds, and the smaller ones, used to locate hares and other small animals, eventually were called Beagles or Bassets.

Worldwide, Beagles' sizes vary greatly, but in American conformation shows, the Beagle stands no more than 15 inches (38 cm) tall and is the smallest of the many scenthound breeds. A smaller variety of the Beagle breed, no taller than 13 inches (35 cm) at the shoulder, is recognized in American Kennel Club

(AKC) classes as well. There are no differences between the two varieties except their height. Beagles share many of the same progenitors as the English Foxhound but are only about half as tall as this larger cousin. They resemble the Foxhound in many ways, as would be expected. These two breeds were developed during the same period in Great Britain for similar purposes, but in spite of the similarity of appearance, the diminutive Beagle is not a miniature Foxhound.

Most references agree that the Beagle was developed to its present type in Great Britain, more specifically in England and Wales. However, scenthounds were bred and used all over the British Isles and on the Western European continent. The exact location of the first hound to resemble the present-day Beagle is unknown.

Talbot

According to some writers, scent dogs known as Talbot hounds were brought into Great Britain by William the Conqueror in the eleventh century and are the likely ancestors of modern Beagles. Beagles of that

While facts surrounding the Beagle's place of origin are sketchy, most agree that the breed was developed in Great Britain.

period may have been known as Kennettys. The now-extinct Talbot has been described as a mostly white scenthound that may have been used to develop the Bloodhound and some of Great Britain's large mastiff-type guard dogs as well. Writers who question the scenting ability of the Talbot have disputed this dog as a Beagle ancestor.

Southern Hound

Southern Hounds were slow-moving, deliberate hunting dogs, developed in the south of England. These deep-voiced scenthounds differed from the North Country Hounds in attitude, size, and speed. The Beagle may have resulted from crossing the Harrier with the old English Southern Hound and maintaining the smallest offspring as Beagle brood stock.

Kerry Beagle

The Kerry Beagle or Pocodan is an Irish dog that is usually black and tan in color and significantly larger than the modern Beagle. It is speculated to have contributed to the gene pool of the early Beagle.

Kerry Beagles are not recognized yet as a specific breed, although in Ireland the breed has thrived for many years and has earned a notable history as a small-game hunter. Kerrys look like lightweight, somewhat smaller versions of the Bloodhound and may be responsible for some of the modern-day Beagles' scenting ability.

In the middle of the nineteenth century, from these various breeds, emerged the modern Beagle, in appearance a solidly built miniature

Foxhound. Beagles are truly one of the earliest recognized scenthound breeds.

The Beagle Name

Scenthounds often were named according to their use, such as Foxhounds or Harriers. However, Beagles probably were named for their size or voice. The name may have come from the French words *béer* (to gape or open wide) and *guele* (throat). The term *Bégueule*, then, would mean to gape or to open the throat widely and might refer to the breed's characteristic baying when afield.

Another French word, *beigle*, means "of little value" and is thought by some to be associated with the name of this breed.

The Celtic word for "small" is *beag*, the Old English word is *begle*, and the French word is *beigh,* all of which are possible origins of this small hound's name.

The term *beagle* seems to have originated in the late 1400s or early 1500s and commonly was used in sixteenth-century English sporting literature. However, *beagle* wasn't used as specific breed's name, but referred to smaller scenthound breed(s).

The word *beagling* isn't found in Webster's dictionary, but it's well-recognized in canine fancy. Used by the Beagle community for practically all endeavors that involve their beautiful dogs, beagling might refer to

hunting squirrels or hares with a favorite Beagle gundog. To another beagler it could mean entry of a Beagle in a field trial on Saturday. Other beagling might include running Beagles in braces, or in small or large packs. Some beaglers are more interested in conformation showing, agility, or obedience trials. That beagling is a bona fide sport can't be questioned when one reviews the number of formal and private field activities involving Beagles.

Beagles are curious, adventuresome creatures.

Beagle pets retain their hunting instincts.

Historical Popularity

In ancient Britain, Beagles originated prior to the rise of Roman domination of Europe. Beagling retained its great favor in the days of King Henry VIII and was even more popular during the reign of his daughter, Elizabeth. The royal court often carried these capable little hunting dogs to the field in their saddlebags. Beagles' size and pack amicability made them the perfect sporting dogs to accompany the queen's court in her progresses about the nation.

While enjoying the fancy of royalty, Beagles also were held in high regard by the general populace. In those early days, Beagles' scenting ability put the breed in demand as tracking dogs. Sportsmen and meat hunters alike kept packs of these active little hounds all across the British Empire.

As a sport in the eighteenth century, hare hunting lost popularity as foxhunting took center stage among English royalty and landed gentry. Long-legged hounds were developed for use in hunting the fleet-footed fox. Kings and queens, lords and ladies dressed in colorful sporting attire and, mounted on spirited jumping horses, joined the chase. Foxhounds were the order of the day; foxhunting on horseback offered more excitement, more speed, and more action than following on foot behind a Beagle pack.

Beagles, however, hardly faded during that time. English farmers maintained small packs of the little hounds and organized both formal and informal hunting forays for sport and to furnish table meat. Beagle packs were especially popular among the English farming community because the short-legged dogs could be followed on foot, eliminating the need for a stable of expensive hunters and jumpers.

About this same period, the pocket Beagle came into popularity. By the early nineteenth century, a Beagle measuring only 8 or 9 inches (20–23 cm) in height was developed to lead less athletic ladies and children on hare hunts. These little dogs possessed fine noses and faithfully held to the trails of their quarry, even though they occasionally had to be carried across particularly rough terrain.

Beagles in America

Beagles rank high in popularity among all dog breeds in this country and are second to the Dachshund in popularity among the hound breeds. The first Beagles were imported to America about 1640. Reported to have resembled straight-legged Dachshunds with weak heads, those Beagles are said to have been good hunters but lacking in beauty and balance. They were apparently best

Beagles were originally gundogs.

known in the southern United States, where they were used to hunt hares, squirrels, and rabbits.

Early in the 1870s, General Rowett of Carlinville, Ohio brought the first contemporary Beagles to the United States. Among those first arrivals were Rosey and Dolly, Beagles that were primarily selected for their hunting ability. The Rowett strain was developed from these dogs and others that arrived shortly thereafter. Through many generations, Beagles of this American strain were in great demand due to their type and natural ability, and because they were small, handy field dogs with enormous hearts.

In ensuing years, more fine Beagles were imported from their native England by American sportsmen and were crossed with the Rowett strain. Early in the twentieth century, beagling became a popular sport in America, having nearly the same formal flavor as British foxhunting. In 1888, the National Beagle Club (NBC) was formed and, on November 3, 1890, held the first Beagle field trial in Hyannis, Massachusetts.

Small Beagle packs have been maintained by thousands of clubs and private citizens all over the country. Competition among these packs has been and is today a popular sport.

Gundog

The Beagle is first of all a gundog. In America, the breed is used extensively for hunting prolific cottontail rabbits, once one of the most prized wild meat sources of this country. Lately, hares, such as the jackrabbit or snowshoe rabbit, are preferred to the quick cottontail that readily goes to ground. These larger hares, although lacking in palatability, are more likely to give the Beagle a longer, faster run and, although the quarry isn't necessarily caught or killed, they are favored.

In various parts of the country, Beagles hunt squirrels and other small mammalian game, and some are quite proficient in pursuit of upland game birds such as pheasants and quail.

Popularity

Because of their pack heritage, hounds were more aloof and less demonstrative than many breeds. Hunting instincts surpassed their owner bonding and they were considered to be only fair companions.

Today, the friendly and gentle Beagle is considered to be one of the finest family pets and companion dogs of any breed. In 1998, the Beagle was the sixth most popular out of 146 breeds registered by the AKC. There were 53,322 Beagles registered, which paled by comparison to the number one breed, the Labrador Retriever, which registered nearly three times that number. The Golden Retriever, German Shepherd Dog, Rottweiler, and Dachshund also scored higher than the Beagle, but their numbers were similar to the Beagle's. Registered Beagle litters placed eighth in 1998 with a total of 21,451.

Beagles ran in 527 AKC field trials, more than any other breed, including retrievers, spaniels, and pointers. Within the hound group, Beagles were awarded 439 Field Champion titles out of the total of 507 awarded for the entire group.

The versatile Beagle isn't just for chasing rabbits. Beagles earned 283 AKC conformation Champion titles, second in the hound group to the Dachshund.

Chapter Three

Who Is This Beagle?

What is the identity of this dog with whom I've decided to share my life? What is the essence of this little hound-colored package of flesh? What do I see when I watch the changing softness of her eyes; do they shift from mischievousness to resolve? Has she a mind of her own; does she think, reason, solve problems, or is she a manufactured, cookie-cutter copy of all other Beagles?

Sam and Rosy

In half the chapters of this book, the Beagle heroine is named *Rosy*. In the other half, a male Beagle named *Sam* takes the starring role. This writing technique is intended to eliminate any hint of sexism and it avoids the use of the clumsy terminology *he or she*. By naming our Beagle, the frequent use of the neutral pronoun, *it,* is eliminated as well. After all, this book is about your new Beagle, a living personality, not an *it*.

Personality

Often we fail to define terms and this oversight impedes understanding. Unfortunately, in many respects, that's the case when discussing personality, attitude, and behavior of dogs. Unquestionably, Rosy has inherited Beagle features that influence her attitude and, thus, to an extent, have a bearing on her behavior, but is that all there is to it?

• Personality is the totality of Rosy's nature, her character, individuality, and personal identity. It is seen in her habits and quality of behavior.

• Attitude is her disposition, inclination, orientation, and temperament. It's Rosy's manner of acting or thinking that influences her makeup.

• Behavior is her bearing, manners, deportment, performance, and way of life. Rosy's behavior is the way she acts or her responses to stimulation.

As you can see, these terms have overlapping definitions that are almost interchangeable. Remember that no two Beagles are alike in spite of the similarity of appearance. Their needs for physical comfort are similar as well, but their individual requirements vary a great deal.

A Happy Beagle

Beagle contentment is at its highest when Rosy lives the role of family member. She's taken for frequent walks and periodically is given the opportunity to pursue her natural trailing instincts.

Perpetual confinement to a kennel will spoil any dog, especially a people-oriented Beagle. However, Beagles have been successfully kenneled when hunted regularly. In this regard, if Rosy is to be confined for long periods, acquire another dog to keep her company.

Hardy and strong, a well-bred Beagle stays in excellent condition with little effort on the part of the owner, but some special circumstances need mentioning. Like any other breed, the cheerful and usually obedient Beagle isn't the dog for every family. Rosy doesn't adapt well to sedentary living, preferring an active, energetic life. If a Beagle is maintained in the absence of other dogs, significant attention must be given to exercise, training, and work. This is true of most breeds, but is doubly important in Beagles. Rosy is quite pack-oriented, craves human and canine society, and does poorly if both are withheld.

Beagles are dogs for all seasons.

Having a long history as dogs that are hunted in packs, Beagles invariably socialize well with other dogs and are equally amiable in family situations. Rosy will adapt to nearly every environment and climate.

In severe winter weather, owners must think of warm housing for the short-coated Beagle, but most of these friendly little hounds will adapt quickly to a life as housedogs during such times. More than a few Beagles are known to warm the feet of their owners during cold winter nights, adding Beagle body heat to that of down comforters. In America today, most Beagles are kept as companion housedogs, in spite of the resurgence of field activities that suit their hunting heritage.

Fun-loving and happy little dogs with a great sense of humor, they are, however, intelligent pets that excel in the companion-dog role.

Stars in Their Own Right

It's a rare Beagle who owns expensive paintings, sleeps atop a doghouse, writes novels, or flies World War I vintage airplanes. This, of course, describes Snoopy, the most famous Beagle of all. Have you ever wondered why Charles Schulz gave Charlie Brown's Beagle that name? Although not confirmed, I believe it's because Beagles always use their noses. Typically, they are snoopy, curious, playful, and mischievous.

Few dog lovers can resist the soft eyes and energetic tongue of a Beagle puppy. Is it any wonder they are popular stars of comic strips and television dog food commercials?

Positive Attributes

Like the comic strip star, Beagles love to play games and are rarely absent from the midst of family gatherings. Often boisterous and playful when young, these gentle charmers are eager to identify with and romp with their children by the hour.

The gentle tolerance of Beagles for children is legendary. A Beagle's loyalty and love for family (and vice versa) is well recognized by Beagle breeders and owners. This breed has earned the reputation of being among the greatest canine companion pets.

Rosy has a rugged body that at the same time is refined and clean-lined. She will display a reserved, almost aloof air of movement and carriage, yet will welcome the advances of friendly strangers. Beagles rarely are trained to act as guard dogs and often will be much too sociable to fill that need.

The Beagle is quick to learn, thrives on attention, and responds to kind words and actions (and a tasty morsel). Training is easily accomplished when Rosy is given tasks that are understood and appropriately rewarded.

A good hunting dog requires great determination above all else. The Beagle possesses this desire to track and is equipped with a keen nose in the bargain. Beagles are known to work out a cold trail under adverse circumstances, concentrating on their memorized scent of the quarry until it is found and identified.

Dogs of this spectacular breed work in rough cover in foul or fair weather, giving their attention to locating their prey without regard to their personal comfort. They have great endurance and stamina, as is proven by hours-long work in field trials in actual hunting conditions.

Questionable Traits

Kathy Forbes of Skyline Beagles comments that Beagles make great kids' companions because they often act just like kids. If you tell your child to go to his room, he will usually procrastinate. A Beagle's response to commands is similar unless you give the command with a tasty treat as a reward for performance. Children and Beagles both require structure in their lives, and without it, you'll probably have trouble.

Cuddly Beagle pups always grow up to demand the continued attention of their human families. Noisy if bored and destructive if neglected, Beagles are nonetheless excellent family pets, but to be appreciated, they must be taught manners, obedience, and social graces.

Unappreciated Characteristics

Instinctive traits that are passed down through generations of hunting dogs form related reasons why you might not appreciate all of your Beagle's behavior. Rosy may have a number of unwanted or unappreci-ated behavioral features that can challenge the most devoted owner. Remember that some inherited characteristics defy all attempts to change. Such is the runaway Beagle.

Patience is a necessity when schooling your Beagle. Obedience training may be going well when confined to your backyard, but when taken off lead outside the fence, Rosy's nose may decide to follow a hot trail, and obedience training takes a backseat to the call of natural instincts.

Although a loyal and attentive family dog, Rosy probably will desert a backyard full of her favorite children in favor of the adventure of a fresh animal track. Trailing propensity is one of the most undesirable characteristics of the breed when Rosy isn't taken afield and is kept as a family pet. It must quickly be recognized that this trait is not always inappropriate and is natural to trail hounds.

The Beagle's distinctive and often loud voice is another objectionable feature. They're equipped with vocal ability to match their keen noses. Happily, this voice keeps their human followers aware of their progress on the trail, and Beagles have been appropriately labeled "the music makers of the meadow." The melody produced by a Beagle pack is a symphony to the ears of sportsmen, who are nearly as proud of this little dog's cocky attitude and appearance as of the music she produces.

Giving voice or tongue is a natural phenomenon that is characteristic of many trail hounds and serves a useful purpose. These sounds allow handlers to locate the pack as well as interpret the freshness of the track they're following.

A single Beagle voice is a mournful yowl that seems to carry forever during the still hours of the night. In a residential setting, this baying may cause sensitive neighbors to resent and even take drastic measures to stop the noise. Although this howl may be discouraged, it is virtually impossible to stop a Beagle from vocalizing. When left alone for extended periods, it's easy to predict that every Beagle will bay.

Behavior

Canine behavior refers to Rosy's deportment, the manner in which she conducts herself. Her behavior may be different in your home from what it was in her previous home or in the whelping nest.

Wolves, wild dogs, and domestic canines share certain common instinctive behavior. Living in human environments for generations has modified that behavior only slightly. Naturally, human habits and personalities influence a dog's behavior, because people set the standards by which a dog's behavior is judged. What is considered normal behavior for your dog in your home may be seen as inappropriate or abnormal in someone else's home.

Canine behavior may be desirable or atrocious, but it is always measured in human society, in human terms, with human rules.

A couple of centuries ago, instinctive canine behavior was more

A Beagle voice is distinctive, if not always welcome.

acceptable, because the dog had a particular purpose, a narrowly defined job to do. The dog of yesteryear lived in a kennel or on a tether, outside the human residence. She was expected only to perform duties that ranged from pulling a sled to retrieving game birds. She might walk in circles all day, turning a spit or other mechanical device. At dusk, guard dogs were loosed on the estate and spent the night making their rounds with a groundskeeper. Each dog had her explicit function, and as long as it was performed satisfactorily, the dog's instinctive behavior was largely ignored.

When the dog evolved to a more important role, that philosophy changed. Worldwide, very few dogs are now performing the function for which they were developed; yet today's dog serves a far more meaningful purpose. Rosy the Beagle is now more than a keen nose, more than a kenneled dog whose job it is to trail small game. She has assumed the role of companion, friend, playmate, and member of her human family. In this expanded role, her behavior is her most important feature. She is expected to relegate canine instincts to the background and accept learned behavior as her norm.

Behavioral Adjustment

Dogs are equipped with a highly malleable character. Through selective breeding, their personalities and behavior, as well as their appearance, often can be altered and molded to suit the owners. Unfortunately, these changes may require many generations of careful selection to amplify certain characteristics and reduce or eliminate others. Sometimes the targeted undesirable characteristic doesn't respond, while other desirable characteristics are lost in the effort.

"Behavior modification" and "adjustment" are terms used to describe a human's attempt to change a dog's behavior from bad to better, from inappropriate to acceptable. Often, the difficulty begins when the owner decides that it's possible to change all behavioral traits.

The key to owning a well-behaved dog is to prevent bad habits from developing and to encourage all desirable behavior. This is begun when Rosy is a tiny puppy, through bonding, training, and conditioning, using rewards and reinforcements.

Analysis of Inappropriate Behavior

You must first decide when, why, and where the inappropriate behavior is seen. Then you can select the necessary adjustment technique to use. Don't attempt to change an undesirable behavior the first time you see it. Make mental notes of the circumstances surrounding each episode, the people involved, and, in particular, the attitude Rosy displays.

Your Role

Behavioral problems are often associated with the dog's lack of confidence in you, the owner, a lack

Mouthing is normal, chewing is a vice.

of respect for your person and possessions. Leadership or dominance problems are the number one reason for behavioral problems (see Dominance Schooling, page 85). This lack of respect sometimes can be reduced or eliminated in the following ways:

• Never respond to a command that is given by Rosy. Except while housebreaking, when she barks, don't jump up and let her out. Wait a few minutes, get a drink of water, pick up a newspaper to scan for a minute. Then open the door.

• Never fail to spend plenty of time playing with Rosy, but be sure *you* pick the time. When Rosy demands attention, ignore her, let her wait until you are ready to pet or play. If she brings her ball for a game of catch, ignore the ball, pick up a brush, and groom her.

• Periodically, when Rosy nudges you for affection, turn and walk away, and ignore her cheeky behavior. After a few minutes, get her retrieving dummy and toss it for her. Give her an obedience command, and after she has correctly performed, reward her with your affection.

No

This word or command undoubtedly is the most overworked term in the average Beagle owner's vocabulary. A cartoon sprang up many years ago: One dog is talking to another and says, "My name's Rover, what's yours?" The second dog answers "I'm not sure, but I think it's No No Bad Dog."

If used at all, *"No"* should be sounded only in emergencies. Perhaps it's appropriate when a muddy-footed Rosy jumps up on your new suit, but if used under those circumstances, be sure she understands what's wrong with her actions. Generally, you should think of other, more specific commands to redirect Rosy's inappropriate behavior.

Chewing or Mouthing

Chewing doesn't result from a wanton desire to destroy your property; it isn't a perverse behavioral characteristic. It's an instinctive trait. Rosy is investigating her environment in the most effective manner she knows.

Chewing is normally seen twice in dogs' lives. It will be at its worst when Rosy is teething. Baby teeth are shed and an adult set erupts between 16 and 28 weeks of age.

If you have prepared well and survived that period, you should be able to withstand the next teething phase. Between six and ten months, she may begin chewing again. This stage is termed the "exploration period" and is the time that Rosy will familiarize herself with her environment by mouthing, tasting, and sampling virtually everything in her path. This stage varies in intensity with the individual dog, and Beagles aren't reported to be any worse than any other breed.

Mouthing is a natural behavior that can't or shouldn't be eliminated from Rosy's experience. Instead, you must learn how to reroute the chewing and focus it on an object that you choose to take the place of your arm, shoe, or baseball glove. Channel Rosy's inherent desire to investigate by substituting safe and interesting toys, food-filled chewies, and hard bones. This technique will work, especially if you remember to praise her when she begins gnawing on an appropriate chew toy.

If you pick up and put away your gloves, belts, purses, shoes, and other attractive items from your wardrobe, you'll reinforce this lesson. Keep these objects well out of Rosy's reach, and never, ever give Rosy a worn-out shoe or other personal item to play with.

Above all, don't scold or punish Rosy's chewing. When you find that she has just reduced your new sneakers to slippery strips of man-made materials, you'll be tempted to reprimand her. True, she looks guilty, but her appearance probably is a submissive countenance brought on by your obvious emotion; you look mad as heck! If you scold, hit, or otherwise punish her, you'll defeat your intention to get and keep her confidence. She won't understand why you scolded her, but will remember only that you are subject to sporadic fits of anger that she must watch for and hopefully escape.

Tug-o-War

Puppies love to grab one end of a rope or knotted sock and race about, wanting to be chased. When caught, they will invariably shake the object, growling and inviting you to take the other end and tug. Beagles are small enough that this game usually is played without problems, but be mindful when playing tug-o-war. Many books and behavioral specialists advise against this game for all dogs. The reason is that the dog becomes increasingly competitive, and each time you play, Rosy will try harder to win the game. In some aggressive breeds, this game can become a competition that tests dog against owner, and a role reversal is seen. In the usual Beagle personality, tug-o-war has no great significance, but you should be aware of the danger.

Toy Selection

You must select the time and the toy for each game and play session. While it's only natural to leave a few toys with Rosy all the time, for instance, a nylon bone or a rawhide chewy, others should be put away when the game is over. Perhaps two toys will be used in a game, such as a rubber bone and a ball. In the game, she will be taught the name of each, but the choice of these toys is yours, not Rosy's.

Rotate toys and games so they are not repeated endlessly. Try to keep something new in store for your Beagle all the time. You'll find her interest will be higher, and her appreciation greater, if she can't predict what game you've scheduled for the session.

Barking

Excessive, inappropriate barking is a behavioral problem that is easier prevented than corrected. A noisy Beagle probably is being left alone too much and is bored with her own company. When still a puppy, a remote negative reinforcement generally will work. When Rosy barks, she gets a squirt of water *in the face*, and she makes the connection quickly.

Often, barking is the only means by which a bored dog can get the

Beagle accessories.

attention of her owner. If you open the door and shout at Rosy, you've given her the reward she knew she would get, your attention. She's no dummy, and even a discouraging word from you is better than being ignored.

Fear of Loud Noises

Beagles are occasionally frightened by the sound of a gun, thunder, or firecrackers. Some are even sensitive to louder than usual household noises such as slamming doors or lawnmower engines.

This problem behavior has no perfect answer, but one technique is used with fair success; it entails a little electronic help. First, you decide which noise Rosy is most frightened of. Then you enlist the aid of a tape recorder to capture the noise. Play the tape over and over and repeat the sound on another recorder until you have a tape full of thunder, lawnmower noises, or gunshots.

Play the tape at a very low volume while playing with Rosy at her favorite game, while she is being groomed, or when she's playing with her yard ball. Choose the activities she enjoys most, and play the record for a few minutes, then discontinue. At the next play session, play the recording again, and so on until she no longer pays any attention to it.

Next, increase the volume a few decibels, and repeatedly play the tape while Rosy is pleasantly occupied. Keep increasing the time she is exposed to the sound, and increasing the volume until she becomes desensitized to the sound. Sooner or later, you will find it necessary to expose her to the actual sound, at a fair distance if possible.

When the fear problem stems from thunder, you obviously have no control over when it occurs, but you can try to desensitize her by playing your thunder recording at night, when Rosy can't perceive the darkening of the sky. If you can accustom her to the sound of thunder, you might win the battle, but most dogs will still run for cover when the sky darkens during the day.

Jumping Up

This behavior is typical, almost instinctive in dogs that have little respect for their people, and is a cry for training. Jumping up is a most undesirable behavior that should be discouraged as early as possible. It's easily stopped without making Rosy uncomfortable, without stepping on her toes or knocking her to the ground with your knee. Shutting her away from you will make the problem worse, but three techniques may work.

• Turn and walk away. Rarely will Rosy jump up on your back. She wants your attention and she's looking for affection. Ignore her for a few minutes, then kneel down and call her to you, scratch her ears and pet her. Tell Rosy she's a good girl; heap praise on her for coming to you.

• In a trained dog that has had some obedience lessons, use the *stop* or *halt* command when Rosy begins to jump, follow immediately with *sit,* then kneel and pet her, rewarding her with praise and treats for her total performance.

• Schooling will always help; busy dogs develop fewer behavioral problems than those that are bored. Enroll Rosy in a puppy kindergarten class. Begin her obedience schooling, take her for walks, play scenting games with her. Make yourself available; give her more attention; make your coming and going more routine and it will have less impact on her.

Aggressiveness and Timidity

The typical attitude of the xenophobic dog (one that is frightened of strangers) is to stand with tail down, ears relaxed, and lips pulled back in a grin. Occasionally fear will cause her to bark, whine, or squat and urinate. Sometimes she will run away, or under certain circumstances, the frightened dog will shy away, then return and bite.

Not usually a Beagle characteristic, timidity often is a precursor to more serious problems. This behavior must be modified quickly.

In some cases, the easiest way to be sure of what a dog is going to do in the company of half a dozen strangers is to crate Rosy before visitors arrive. Place her kennel near the center of the seated people and, after a few moments, open the crate. Everyone remains in position, and as she glances at each, they speak to her in quiet tones and offer her treats from their hands. This is sometimes referred to as a flooding technique,

and it isn't the easiest method of handling the irrational fear of strangers.

The best behavioral adjustment for timidity is to ask some friends for help; select two or three people who haven't met Rosy. Ask one to ring your doorbell, and when you've answered the door, shake hands with the new arrival and speak briefly with him, introducing Rosy by name. By this time, Rosy probably will be hiding behind you, uncertain of her role. The stranger slowly kneels down and speaks to Rosy without reaching for her. He offers her a special treat from an open palm while continuing to speak softly to her, then stands and leaves.

This exercise is repeated two or three times until Rosy begins to anticipate the bell and watch for the stranger's treat. The next day, another stranger rings your bell, and the same routine is followed.

When Rosy becomes less shy, the strangers can offer a treat with one hand while extending the other with an open palm to touch her cheek, gradually advancing to scratching her chin, and so forth.

Make a practice of having some delectable treats ready for anyone to use when they come to visit. Warn friends ahead of time of the behavioral adjustment underway, and ask their cooperation.

Depending on the severity of the problem, you may be able to stop this program when Rosy has become accustomed to strangers coming to your home. If you wish, you can go further with this adjustment to include

Typical posture of intimidated dogs.

a stranger who makes up to Rosy, snaps on her leash, and takes her for a brief walk punctuated by frequent yummy treats.

Rosy must come to realize that people she previously hasn't met aren't to be treated with disdain. Your objective is to teach her that she should relax when you have met and greeted strangers courteously and have invited them in. Be sure that friends participating in this program understand the problem. They must wait for your introduction and should speak quietly to the dog, using her name frequently. They must take their time, never jerk their hands back when she moves to take the treat, and never stare into her eyes.

Urinary Soiling

Analysis also is extremely important in this situation.

• Be certain *you* aren't the problem. If you ever yell at Rosy or stare into her eyes to intimidate her, stop it! A clue to fright urination is Rosy's body posture. Does she cower or squat when she urinates? Dogs don't understand grudges so, if she made a mistake yesterday, she can't be expected to remember it today. Obviously, if you're the cause, you must also be the cure.

• Consider your housebreaking techniques and prepare to modify them. Do you punish her in any way? Dogs have an uncanny ability to interpret the moods of their owners. Are you getting her out to the toilet area regularly and frequently?

• Does she have a urinary tract infection? If Rosy has an inflamed bladder or bladder stones, she may lose bladder control. Clues to this problem are foul or rank urine, dark, thickened, or bloody urine, straining to urinate, and frequent urinary necessity while passing only minute amounts. The answer to urinary infection or stones lies with Rosy's veterinarian, who should be called immediately.

• Does Rosy urinate in particular places? She may be marking instead of urinating. Marking is an instinctive behavior that is used to designate territory. It's usually done outside, but when a housedog marks, often it's near a window or in another place where Rosy can see a strange dog in her domain.

Marking is intended to ward off interlopers and thereby prevent actual combat to protect a territory. A wise dog will mark as her territory only that which she feels she can defend, which, unfortunately, may be your living room.

Marking often is associated with lack of confidence. If Rosy isn't self-confident in her environment, she may mark. If quite relaxed in her environment, she is less apt to mark. Outside, a confident dog will mark the perimeter of her yard and a timid dog will mark nearer to her house.

Rosy's veterinarian may use hormone therapy to treat urinary marking behavior or, in the case of male dogs, castration may be beneficial.

Timidity can be reduced by socialization—meeting new people and dogs—and by giving your Beagle more attention—spending more time with her and showing your approval each time she overcomes strange situations.

• Is Rosy's urine found where she has been lying, or does she soil her coat? In those cases, the urine leakage may have hormonal causes, or it may be an indication of a metabolic disease. In either case, she should be examined by her veterinarian.

• When Rosy is quite old, she actually may forget her training. Canine cognitive dysfunction is the term used to describe this old dog memory loss. Some of the new memory drugs may be of value, but a physical examination should first be performed to rule out other causes. Often, this condition will respond to regular, scheduled trips to the toilet area, frequent walks, and praise when she urinates in appropriate places.

• If Rosy urinates each time she meets a stranger on the street, it may be a sign of submission. Usually, submissive dogs will urinate when approached by strangers or other dogs, and anytime they are unsure of themselves. Therapy for this behavior is to instruct friends to ignore Rosy and not to reach for her or speak to her. If she's young, enroll her in a puppy kindergarten to help build self-confidence. Desensitize or accustom her to other dogs by frequent walks on streets where other dogs can be seen but are behind fences or on leashes.

Coprophagia, or Feces Eating

This disgusting behavior is more common in kenneled dogs than in those that are given more freedom. It may be seen when Rosy is a tiny puppy, or it may appear at a later time. Once again, the solution to this problem follows proper analysis. Does she eat her own feces or that of other animals? Does she consume the excreta when she is hungry or when bored? Sometimes this is difficult to determine because Beagles always act hungry.

Theories abound relative to coprophagia. Some say dogs eat the feces of other dogs to destroy those dogs' territorial marking. Another explanation is that coprophagia is associated with boredom, and yet others speculate that this ugly habit is related to a nutritional enzyme deficiency. Others say the dog is copying other dogs: monkey see, monkey do.

Or, coprophagia may be due to the delectable taste of poop. Yum Yum! The basis for this theory is plausible; as revolting as eating cat manure may sound, cats have higher protein requirements than dogs, and their foods usually contain more protein. Therefore, cat feces contain more protein wastes and partially digested protein, and it may be tastier. Yuck!

Still another theory might be offered. Wolves often eat the stomach and intestinal contents of their kill before consuming the muscle. That instinctive behavior may be inspired by their need for fibrous vegetable roughage in their diet. Herbivores' bulky feces reflect their vegetarian diets and are flavored with green foods. Dogs that are attracted to greens may actually crave these pasture puddings.

Should it be necessary, treatment should begin by consulting with Rosy's veterinarian. If she can detect no nutritional deficiency or other reason for the behavior, carry a can of cayenne pepper to spread on her feces or the cat's and other animals' excretions. Other more scientific products are available; some work, others are hoaxes. Adding brewer's yeast tablets to her diet sometimes will stop Rosy from eating her own feces, but the reason for this remains a mystery.

Coprophagia is sometimes caused by boredom.

Rolling in Feces or Carcasses

Dogs instinctively roll in the excretions or carcasses of other species, another sex, or another social rank. This nasty behavior may be impossible to correct and is due to Rosy's desire to mask her own odor with that of another animal. It's rather like donning camouflage.

Tonguing

Hidden above a dog's hard palate is a little tubular structure called the vomeronasal organ (VNO). It is lined with nerve cells that carry a signal directly to the brain; it's truly a sixth sense.

The VNO opens by way of a tiny aperture between her incisor teeth and her upper lip and allows Rosy to *taste* her environment. With the VNO, Rosy can sense other dogs' pheromones, which are communication chemicals related to sexual and social behavior. It's unknown whether this organ aids in interpretation of the pheromones of other species, but speculation leans toward that possibility.

Begging

This behavior should never be allowed to develop. The first time Rosy begins sniffing around the kitchen while the cook is preparing dinner, the hungry little hound should be confined to her crate or to another room. Don't punish her; when you confine her, give her a stuffed chewy or her nylon bone.

Separation Anxiety

Separation anxiety in the Beagle is probably associated with the breed's instinctive pack desire. Rosy is perfectly happy when in the company of her pack, but when the pack leaves and she's left behind, she may panic within a few minutes.

She becomes terrified and begins to destroy her environment, especially doors. Sometimes she urinates, defecates, cries, howls, or whimpers. She isn't being bad; she is actually quite uncomfortable in her family's absence. Probably, she suffers as much when you're gone as you do when you return to find the house in shreds.

To alter this behavior, leave for short but increasing periods of time. Each time you leave the house, tell her "Rosy, wait." At first, leave only for a few minutes, later, half an hour, then an hour, and so forth. When you leave, always tell her the same thing, and don't make a big production out of your going or your return. Simply enter, greet her with a brief scratch, and begin doing something unrelated to the dog.

Try not to associate leaving or returning with a particularly enjoyable playtime with your Beagle. In other words, don't play catch with her immediately before or after your outings.

Increase Rosy's exercise. Take her for walks, even short ones, periodically through the day and especially an hour or so before leaving. Try to tire her out so she'll be ready for a nap when you leave.

Give her a long-lasting treat such as a food-stuffed hollow chew toy. These food-hiding toys are of various colors and construction. All have a common characteristic—they hold food, and the dog must learn how to get to it. (Unless you like cleaning up after such a device is used, only put dry dog foods inside.)

Some Beagles are taught to sleep in their kennels or crates, and if Rosy has a crate that she appreciates as a den, try crating her while you're away. Never leave her without some mark of your affection, such as an item of your clothing that hasn't been washed and a rawhide chew stick, a food-filled toy, or another time-occupying object.

Cat Chasing

Beagles often track cats; cats don't like being followed and that causes Tommy to run with Rosy in

Face licking is normal between friendly dogs.

hot pursuit. This behavior is understandable but isn't the easiest situation to cope with in a family setting.

The best corrective technique is to introduce the cat under controlled circumstances. Put Rosy on a short leash. Another family member brings in the new cat and, about the time Rosy begins to fidget, you slip her a particularly tasty treat, accompanied by petting. As she settles down, praise her and give another treat.

If the cat is established first as a family pet, crate Rosy and allow the resident cat to investigate. When Rosy becomes bored with the crate, take her out on a leash and heap on praise and treats as she learns to tolerate the feline resident. If the cat wants to play, and initiates a game of chase, don't stop the pup, but try to be on hand when the game is over. Be sure the cat has access to an elevated safe space to which she can escape if necessary. Feed your feline and canine pets at different times, in different places.

Face Licking

Face licking is an instinctive behavior stemming from Rosy's nest experiences. She licked her mother when she wanted attention or food. She licked her siblings and pack mates to show submission or affection. You're the alpha member of her human family, her mother figure, and her pack mate, and you must tolerate the licking. Don't fight it. It isn't everyone who has the exceptionally good fortune to own a Beagle with a busy tongue.

Chapter Four

Picking the Best Beagle

Type of Beagle

Puppy selection should represent an honest attempt to match your ownership qualifications to the needs of the individual dog you're considering.

Before choosing your Beagle, determine what you expect of this dog. If you have the desire to exhibit him in conformation shows, obedience trials, field trials, or other AKC-sponsored events, you should start with a dog from a kennel that has produced winners in whatever event(s) you're interested in.

If you're seeking a companion, a family pet, or a child's pet and have no aspirations of winning blue ribbons, you'll find more to choose from. Every Beagle kennel produces more pets than show or competition dogs. The differences between pet-quality and show-quality Beagles are often quite subtle, and not easily recognized by amateurs. Don't be in a hurry; look around. Ask Beagle breeders to point out the positive and negative characteristics of available pups.

Pets will usually be neutered by maturity, but show dogs and some competition Beagles are kept intact (unneutered). Registered Beagles, whether neutered or not, including oversize dogs and dogs with other noncrippling faults can compete in AKC obedience trials, 4-H obedience, Frisbee contests, tracking trials, and agility trials, as well as the AKC-sponsored Canine Good Citizen program and some non-AKC field trials and gundog contests.

Are You Ready for a Hound?

A conversation I overheard outside the window of a mall pet shop went something like this. A young woman was speaking to her husband. "Isn't that puppy just darling? I love dogs! It's time our kids had a pet, and I'm going to buy that precious little Beagle puppy. He looks just like Snoopy. They'll love him. Look at him, isn't he the most adorable puppy you ever saw? I just want to pick him up and squeeze him! If the shop takes credit cards that puppy will be Tyler's birthday present. After all, our son will be seven years old next week, and he needs some responsibilities. Caring for a pup will teach him just that!"

The worst thing about most American pet shops is that often they are located in malls; we're shopping for shoes and they catch us off guard. Any purchase made on impulse will likely turn out to be disappointing and regretted. While it's true that most families aren't complete without a pet of some kind, Beagles make poor spontaneous purchases.

Shopping for a Beagle should begin only after you and your family have read about and considered the personality and characteristics of many breeds. After settling on a Beagle, keep in mind that no two Beagles are alike, although similarities of individuals within the breed outweigh differences. Before you shop, consider a few general aspects of Beagle ownership.

Ask yourself if you really want a hound, one that loves to yodel in the night, one that has earned the nickname "music maker of the meadows, the sound of which will thrill the most sophisticated owner." A Beagle is a trail hound, one that takes off on the track of every new scent and is quite comfortable joining other dogs to form a hunting pack. Do you want a small, independent-thinking dog, one that hasn't much reputation as a guard dog, one that will probably require many tedious hours of obedience training? Are you well-suited for

the management of a dog that is keen on spending his days tracking rabbits, squirrels, birds, and almost any other creature?

Just when you think you've considered all the negatives, and your mind is made up to buy a puppy of another breed, you hear a story like this one from Ruth Darlene Stewart of Aladar Beagles.

The recent death of Ms. Stewart's mother cast a pall over the evening. Her sister was visiting and decided to stay overnight, but, being in a melancholy mood, asked if she could share Darlene's king-size bed. As the two ladies prepared to retire, her sister asked Darlene what the baby monitor beside the bed was for. Darlene responded that it was tuned to the Beagle kennel and not to be alarmed if barking was heard during the night.

They turned off the light, but Sandy, Darlene's little bed Beagle, was restless. She rooted around, jumped from the bed, whined, and begged for help. Lights on, Darlene saw what was bothering Sandy. It seems this bed Beagle slept with a stuffed duck every night, and it was missing. Later, the duck retrieved, everyone settled down for a nice snooze.

Within minutes, the sisters spontaneously began giggling; a pair of grown women with a Beagle monitor beside the bed and a bed Beagle that couldn't go to sleep without a fuzzy duck. All this in the home of a lady who wanted no children because they were too much trouble!

Time for Your Beagle

Be sure *you* have time to spend with your Beagle. Unfortunately, the personal time factor frequently is overlooked, especially if young children are in the family and little Tyler needs a companion this very minute!

Before a puppy is chosen, give thought to the instinctive habits of the Beagle. Do you have the patience to spend hours teaching your Beagle? Are you short-tempered and easily frustrated, or can you overlook a few stubborn traits in your dog? Will you be angry the first time your Beagle escapes from the yard and runs away in pursuit of a game trail? Are you prepared to Beagle-proof your property and keep your pet confined? Can you accept the baying of your trail hound, or does the sound irritate you? Will you take time from your schedule to play with and exercise your Beagle, or do you intend to delegate these duties to other family members?

Children grow up too fast, and dogs live 12 to 15 years. Some kids have the desire and capability to train and care for a dog while others refuse to accept this responsibility. When the child is seven years old and Sam is a puppy, these chores are okay. Will the picture be as pleasant in six years when the Beagle is in his prime but Tyler is a teenager? Dog care is a major responsibility; it's an assignment that shouldn't arbitrarily be awarded to a youngster.

Necessary Facilities

The Beagle will undoubtedly share your home but will need a section of the yard that is dedicated as a toilet area during and after Sam's housebreaking period. Another need is an easily cleaned spare room or bathroom in which to confine the pup while housebreaking.

If you travel frequently, you should locate a friend or family member to act as your Beagle caregiver. The daily fee and location of an appropriate boarding kennel should be investigated as well.

If you don't have a securely fenced yard, be sure you're prepared to walk Sam on lead several times per day regardless of the weather.

Monetary Considerations

Do you know the average price of a Beagle? In addition to this initial expenditure, the cost of preventive health care and, possibly, insurance

"Let's get this straight; I put it in this can?"

fees should be determined. Veterinary fees should be investigated, including those for routine examinations, annual vaccinations, and worm treatments. Get quotes for the cost of spaying a female or neutering a male. Tick and flea prevention is another item to consider and should be discussed with a veterinarian.

Your Beagle shouldn't live on scraps; Sam deserves a good quality dog food. What is the best food, and what is the annual cost for this food? Don't forget the cost of dishes, beds, collars, leashes, toys, and chewies.

If you're planning a show or performance role for your Beagle, you must think of training assistance. Will you need the help of a professional trainer for field trials, obedience, agility, or show-dog training? Don't forget to add the handler's fee and the cost of entry fees and travel.

Patience

The love and companionship you receive from Sam will more than compensate for the cost of Beagle ownership. However, determination and great patience are definite assets! A quick temper that flares easily isn't compatible with Beagle ownership.

Schooling

Beagles need to be taught essential good manners and basic obedience. At the very least, your Beagle must accept schooling in such common social graces as housebreaking, collar and leash wearing, and some fundamental obedience work. An untrained, unresponsive

hound will be an embarrassment to your household and a detriment to the neighborhood.

When to Buy

Acquire your Beagle at a time when all family members have time to spend with the pup. Don't bring Sam home immediately before the holidays or his needs might be lost in the confusion. If you are contemplating the puppy as a Christmas present, think again! Wait until after the confusion of the season is past, relatives have gone home, and your family has settled into its normal routine.

Immediately prior to a family vacation is another poor time to bring your Beagle home. Transferring Sam's care to a stranger before housebreaking and other early training is complete is a mistake. Even if the caregiver is wise and discriminating, the technique will differ and confuse the puppy.

Puppy

Most lasting relationships between humans and their Beagles begin with puppies. To miss the exuberant natural affection that comes from a Beagle pup is like eating a banana split without the fudge. Beagle babies are the cuddliest pups you'll ever find. They come equipped with soft coats, fast tongues, warm, loving eyes, and a playful temperament.

Owning an eight-week-old Beagle puppy is an adventure. Characteristically, Beagles are so affectionate

Puppy or Adult

You should consider the age of the dog that will best meet your needs. Probable benefits and disadvantages to acquiring a puppy or an adult are briefly listed below.

Puppy	Adult
Bonds quickly with family	Slower to bond
Small, fragile bones	Stronger, more durable
Greater initial expense	Less cash outlay
Housebreaking headaches	May already be housebroken
Disease-susceptible	More disease-resistant
Initial vaccinations	Already vaccinated
Booster vaccination expense	Booster vaccination expense
Short attention span	May catch on easier
More fun for kids	May not be as playful
Chews everything	Hopefully past chewing stage
Train to suit yourself	Must deal with prior training
Expense of spaying/neutering	May already be spayed/neutered
Housing restricted	More latitude in housing

that Sam will capture your heart. Full of fun, high-spirited, and curious, he will gambol about clumsily, falling over his feet and ears. He'll follow you everywhere, getting underfoot at every step, rarely roaming more than a few yards from your presence. When momentarily lost or misplaced, his mournful hound voice will tell you of his displeasure. Your Beagle's first few nights away from his nest and siblings will be evenings to be treasured for years.

Petting and wrestling with Sam are going to be fun for the children of the family, but great care must be taken to assure that Sam doesn't get the worst of these encounters. The Beagle is a small dog; puppy bones break easily, and puppy character is

formed by the early treatment he receives. Children and pups alike must be carefully monitored when together. Toddlers must be taught that Sam should be left on the floor, to be picked up and carried only by older family members.

Housebreaking is a particularly tedious and exasperating time for puppy owners. Days or sometimes weeks are spent running to and from the toilet area of the yard in the middle of the night. Messes must be meticulously cleaned up to avoid future accidents caused by the odors of past mistakes.

Like puppies of all breeds, Beagle pups are subject to diseases and prone to mischief not usually associated with adult dogs. Sam should be checked for worms periodically. Vaccinations are needed, boosters must be given, and the pup's diet will need changing as he matures.

You must puppy-proof your home to accommodate the youthful, sharp-toothed little furniture chewer. Spaying or neutering represents an additional health care expense of puppy ownership.

Adult Beagle

The possibility of acquiring an adult Beagle may appeal to you. Mature Beagles are often available from dog pounds, shelters, and rescue agencies. Other adult Beagles may be obtained from Beagle breeders who have an older adult in good health, one that has had his opportunity in dog shows or field trials and is ready to retire to a nice home.

Adopting an adult Beagle carries slight risk.

Contact Beagle rescue groups and local dog shelters. Give them your name and telephone number and you probably won't wait very long for a dog.

Regardless of the circumstances, don't adopt a mature Beagle without return privileges. Take Sam on trial for at least two weeks, or better yet for a month. Make a promise to yourself to give him every opportunity to adjust to your home, and hold true to your promise. Don't expect miracles, but do expect a stable attitude and the beginning of obedience. If at the end of his probationary period he's making the necessary adjustments, welcome him to your family circle.

A grown Beagle may fit into your life quite easily due to the friendly nature of the breed. However, some adult Beagles have never been taught manners, some lack house-training, and a few have been abused or neglected, which makes their adoption more risky.

A person who's ready to give personal time, love, attention, and patient handling is likely to succeed with an older Beagle. Trust between human and Beagle is the key. When Sam realizes that you're consistent, usually will reward a desirable response, and always will ignore his errors, the game is half won.

When adopted from rescue agencies or shelters, Beagles that have reached maturity usually have well-developed habits, both good and bad. Some will have undesirable personality traits as well. Don't be dismayed. With the exception of instinctive behavior, habits can be altered. Adjustment to a new family with different restrictions and a different lifestyle will naturally take a bit longer than if you were beginning with a puppy.

Dog-owning expense should be lower when you start with a grown Beagle, because Sam probably will come to your home vaccinated and possibly neutered. Adult Beagles generally are stronger and more resistant to infectious diseases than puppies and fewer trips to the veterinarian can be expected.

An adult Beagle probably can live outdoors if a warm doghouse is provided, but he'll bond to you and your family more quickly if kept indoors, especially in the evenings and at night.

If you reach the end of Sam's probationary period and find that he's taken everything you've offered and hasn't softened his bad habits a bit, give it up. An occasional dog's behavior is so indelibly imprinted on his brain, you can spend the rest of his life working with him and still suffer defeat. However, if Sam is beginning to focus his attention on you and is responding to his name and simple commands, you probably have it made.

Male or Female

Sex usually isn't a determining factor when choosing a companion Beagle that will be neutered at or before puberty. Either sex should be easily trained, health-care costs are about the same, and no appreciable differences are seen unless you've decided to buy a breeding-quality animal.

If you are considering entering Sam in conformation show classes or field trials, AKC rules eliminate spaying or castration. You can enjoy AKC tracking, obedience, agility, and other competition with a neutered Beagle.

Beagles are pack dogs and are considered to be quite social; in fact most Beagles thrive on their membership in human or dog packs. Sometimes a new male may present a problem when introduced into an older male's home, but usually this is a mild, temporary disagreement, especially if the dogs are allowed to hunt or run together. Females generally are gentler than males, but this too is relative and varies between individuals.

Purchase of a breeding-quality female presupposes your intention to show and breed her. Well-bred males may win ribbons, trophies, and championship points, but not many are good enough to be considered stud dogs. Purchase of a breeding-quality bitch represents a significant cash outlay that is only the beginning of costs associated with breeding and raising high-quality puppies.

You must remember that a breeding bitch brings other baggage as well. Her heat cycle repeats for about three weeks twice a year, during which times she must be protected from unwanted suitors. Her bloody discharge must be dealt with, and her mood swings while in heat may affect her personality.

Age of the Pup

If you have the opportunity to watch a litter from birth till weaning, you'll observe that the time is spent learning nest etiquette. Until about seven weeks old, Sam is taught what may be done and what brings quick reproof from his dam. He will learn which of his siblings to challenge and which to leave alone. During this time, handle him several times daily if you can, but don't deprive him of this canine socialization. This seven-week period spent with siblings and dam provides his introduction to canine society.

The most important human-puppy bonding period extends from birth to about three months of age. Make every effort to bring Sam into your home as soon as possible after weaning. From 7 to 12 weeks of age is the best time for him to learn to trust and to depend upon you and other humans to supply his needs. If acquired during that time, Beagle pups usually can be housebroken and taught proper manners by eight to ten weeks of age. A word of caution; this is also the period when bad habits are easily learned, and these too are deeply ingrained.

A puppy that receives no human socialization and is only accustomed to his canine family during his first several months of life is likely to present a problem later. He may be shy and slow to bond with his new owners. Beagles are notably sociable little hounds, and this is less a problem with them than with other breeds.

One key to bonding with an older Beagle pup is to be sure the pup receives only positive responses to his actions. Make every effort to *prevent* errors so you won't need to correct them. Be exceptionally generous with praise and petting when any little task is accomplished properly, and always ignore his mistakes.

Temperament and Disposition

Beagle puppies observed in a litter setting may appear as alike as peas in a pod, and it takes careful evaluation to reveal subtle individual differences in temperament. You might see evidence of a little more aggressiveness, mischief, or curiosity in one pup than another. Perhaps one pup may express a shy expression when a noise is heard or a strange face presents itself.

One method to estimate a puppy's future attitude is to observe and handle his dam and sire. Personable parents usually produce friendly puppies. Timidity in a Beagle dam or sire may produce shy puppies that probably won't be the best choice for you. Although it's unlikely that you will find Beagle parents that are shy, aggressive, or belligerent, if you run across them, keep on running.

Beagle pups appear as alike as peas in a pod.

It's easy to choose a happy Beagle; how can you miss? Pick one that wants to know you better, one that responds to you and follows you. Mischievousness is standard for the breed. If you are able, choose a pup that is laid back and less aggressive than others.

Finding the Right Breeder

Thanks to the computer, beaglers are easy to locate today, but finding a reputable breeder is still a challenge. When looking for an important contact, such as the person who has the best Beagle for you, don't risk calling a stranger. Web sites, after all, are similar to the yellow pages. There is no assurance that all Beagle breeders who are listed on the various web sites are equal. In addition to searching the Web for local breeders, go to the AKC web page to locate the National Beagle Club Secretary. (See Useful Addresses and Literature, page 193.)

A personal approach is better. Go to a nearby dog show, obedience trial, agility contest, or field trial to meet other beaglers. The computer may eventually take the place of all such research, but it's best to obtain a breeder referral from your local AKC all-breed club or the National Beagle Club to find the names of reputable breeders near you.

Don't settle on the first breeder you find, the one with the biggest ad, or the one that is closest to your home. As with physicians, lawyers, and veterinarians, advertisements aren't an indication of expertise.

Select a beagler with a good reputation, one who is producing winning dogs. You should see evidence of the breeder's track record in the show or field trial circuit as well as in the appearance and personality of pups offered for sale.

Beagle Cost

A Beagle puppy that has excellent or good potential for a show or field competition career may cost several times the price of a companion pet. If such showing is your bag, obtain your Beagle from a breeder with a history of producing winning dogs and expect to pay accordingly. Companion Beagles are easier on the wallet because the percentage of companions in any litter is much greater. Remember, these dogs come from the same kennels and the same parents as field and show competitors; they are just blessed with fewer desirable physical attributes.

Newspaper Ads

The most desirable Beagle isn't always advertised in the Sunday paper. Amateur or backyard breeders often use this medium to publicize their dogs. If you decide to scan the paper, ask some pertinent questions before you look at puppies. Ask the ages of the parents and make sure they're both registered. If either parent is quite young, be especially careful about hip and eye certification (see Hereditary Diseases, page 161). These less expensive Beagles may turn out to be good companions, but it's extremely unlikely you will locate a fine-quality Beagle among the puppies in a backyard-bred litter.

Puppy Factories

Puppy-mill pups pose a greater danger; these mass-produced Beagles rarely are of reasonable quality. When you go to see a puppy factory litter, the dam is often absent. If you insist on seeing her, an excuse is usually made and, if you persist, she may be thin and in pitiful nutritional condition. A puppy mill is usually filled with dogs of various breeds housed in crowded, dirty kennels with very little provision for exercise. Beagles from puppy mills should be avoided.

Pet Shops

Today's marketing processes often lead you to a well-stocked pet shop in the mall. Although many pet-quality Beagles are obtained from these shops, pitfalls may be found in your path. Pet-shop pups may be younger than those obtained from reputable breeders and this may affect their personality. Another drawback to these pups is the lack of ability to see and handle their parents or siblings. Sometimes pedigrees and pictures of parents are available, and that helps your selection. You may learn the name of the kennel that raised the pup and thus satisfy your need. Yet another pet-shop pup problem relates to hereditary defects and temperament problems of the parents, which often can't be investigated without knowledge of the kennels that raised these individuals.

Look at the Parents

Siblings aren't clones; no two puppies have identical personalities, conformation, or color. Even coat texture varies among pups in the same litter. Puppies may physically resemble each other or have mannerisms that are more similar to one than the other, but each puppy is an individual. The genetic composition of a pup is a mixture of the genes of both parents. In fact, Sam may inherit all the best or worst characteristics of each parent, but probably he will posses a mixture of good and bad genetic features.

A pair of Beagles that display excellent noses and hunting talents will likely produce good hunters, but not always. The same holds true of conformation dogs. If Sam's sire isn't owned by the dam's kennel, you will probably have to settle for seeing his picture and hopefully pictures and accomplishments of his past progeny.

A Healthy Pup

Regardless of whether you buy a show-quality Beagle or a companion, a pack Beagle or a gundog, good health should be your first concern. If you feel inadequate evaluating the health of a pup, don't hesitate to leave a significant down payment and take the pup to a veterinarian for a prepurchase examination. If you decide to go it on your own, you should still take the pup to a veterinarian for a professional checkup

A happy Beagle from a happy environment.

Guarantee or not, this one is mine!

within 24 hours of the purchase time. The fee for such an examination is negligible when compared to a heart murmur that isn't discovered until age three.

A few axioms should be remembered when evaluating the health of your new Beagle pup.

• The best pup in a puny, sick litter isn't good enough. Don't select the best pup from a poor litter of Beagles displaying patchy skin, runny eyes, coughing, skinny bodies, splayed feet, crooked legs, or lethargy.

• Feeling sorry for a pup is a poor excuse for buying him. Remember, Sam will be with you for a long, long time. If he isn't robust when purchased, he may never be sound.

• Never buy a pup that is receiving medication. A reputable breeder won't guarantee that he will be better in a couple of days and would never sell such a pup to you until he's completely recovered.

• Housing and environment should give you a clue about how a breeder has cared for his Beagles. Fresh stools may dot any yard where a litter of puppies is housed, but flies, poor sanitation, dirty coats, and leftover feed in dirty bowls are signs of neglect.

• Look for a fresh water supply and well-nourished, reasonably fat, robust pups with shiny, soft coats and playful attitudes.

Picking the Best Pup

The problem with selecting the best pup from a litter of five or six healthy Beagles is that all of them will compete for your attention and want to go home with you. This breed is universally outgoing and friendly. You aren't likely to frighten them if they have been socialized even a little, but take no chances as you approach them.

• Watch the litter through a window, or slip quietly into their yard and stand against the wall to observe them for a few minutes.

• Watch for aggressiveness; note the most timid puppy, and don't pick a timid Beagle. Shy puppies are often too young to leave the nest or are not well socialized.

• Get down to their level. Sit on the floor or ground, and let the Beagles come to you. Even if you only stand

5-feet tall, your towering height may make them overly cautious.

• Throw a paper wad or small toy away from the pups and observe which one reaches it first and what he does with it. If he brings it to you, you've probably found your Beagle.

• Rig a noisemaker before visiting the litter. A soda can with a few marbles or pennies inside works well. When the pups are interested in the paper wad you've thrown, shake the can and roll it across the lawn. A courageous Beagle will first check the origin of the sound when you shake it and, when you roll it, he will pursue it to investigate. Conversely, lack of self-confidence is displayed by a pup that runs away or hides when the can is shaken.

• Choose a Beagle puppy that is a bit laid back, curious, investigative, and perhaps a little mischievous, but not one that is overtly aggressive or displays a domineering attitude.

• Hyperactive puppies that act as if their spring is wound too tightly often are difficult to train and may make poor companions.

• In a rare instance, you might find a defensive Beagle pup. If he snaps, cries, or tucks his tail and hides, leave him for someone else. He may grow out of this defensive trait with time and handling, but don't take a chance.

Handle the Pup

Allow the pups to climb on your lap, pet them, and, finally, when you have observed them for several minutes, pick up Sam. Hold him close, stand, and walk with him into the house or into another room. When you're alone with him, again sit on the floor and place him beside you. If he's typical, in an instant he'll be all over you, licking at one end and wagging at the other.

Hold him on his back in your arms for a few minutes while you rub his tummy. If he allows this with no crying or excessive squirming, he's probably a good choice.

Look for Congenital Faults

Feel Sam's abdomen for signs of an umbilical hernia. His belly should be smooth, with no protrusions. If you feel a bubblelike soft mass the size of a small marble, it's probably a hernia. When turned on his back, a small hernia usually will disappear. The small hernia may require surgical repair in the future, or it may be inconsequential. Larger hernias usually can be corrected for a modest fee when Sam is neutered.

His testicles should be descended into the scrotum by weaning age. If you can't find them in place, mention it to the breeder and discuss it with your veterinarian when he is taken in for his checkup. Small puppies' testicles frequently are found in the scrotum one day and aren't present the next. This appearance and disappearance of scrotal testicles may be normal until the pup is several months old. However, if you are purchasing Sam as a show or breeding prospect, be sure both testicles are in the scrotum and, if in doubt, have him examined by your veterinarian.

Puppy Records

When you've made your selection and arranged for payment, ask to see Sam's registration and health documents. Among them are the following.

• His AKC puppy registration application should be there, together with a copy of his pedigree.

• His vaccination record should be present, showing when and by whom his immunizations were administered, what product(s) were given, and when the next vaccination is due.

• Results and date of his last fecal examination, together with the name of the deworming product used if the sample was positive should be included.

• If he's seen a veterinarian, the name of his doctor and the reason for his visit should be specified. If he was treated for an illness, the medication used should also be given.

• Dietary information should be written, including the specific diet being fed, the amount, and the frequency of feeding.

• The contract or agreement between you and the breeder. All considerations should be written on this paper, including your agreement to have Sam neutered and the age at which this must be done. If the breeder guarantees Sam's health, it should be specified in the agreement. In case he is found to have some congenital deformity, the contract should state if you are entitled to your money back or a replacement pup.

Chapter Five

Getting to Know Your Beagle

A New Home for Rosy

Plan her homecoming carefully. Don't get anyone else into the act for the first hour or two. It's best to bring her home when the rest of the family is away for a few hours. Immediately upon her arrival, take Rosy to the designated toilet area of the yard. Stay there quietly while she sniffs this area and possibly urinates or defecates before she is taken into the house.

If Rosy is a tiny puppy, she should be allowed to sniff and investigate her new home, one room at a time, under strict supervision. Before being housebroken, Beagle puppies aren't too discriminating when defecating or urinating, and you'll regret allowing her to roam about at will. Follow her around as she checks all corners and hidey-holes, and when you can't be with her, keep her in a pen, crate, or small room until her toilet habits are trustworthy. (See Housebreaking, page 86.)

Your fenced backyard should be next on the agenda. Allow Rosy to sniff around, but close shed and garage doors until you're sure those areas are safe and free from puppy traps.

Puppy-proofing Your Home

Most homes, even those with youngsters toddling about, are full of puppy traps. Beagle puppies are chewers and chewing can get a pup in big trouble!

Curiosity may make this Beagle sick.

"Look what I caught—a long-tailed mouse!"

Unplug electric cords that hang within Rosy's reach and coil them well above her grasp. Chewing on a plugged-in cord may burn her mouth or possibly electrocute her. Even unplugged cords can be dangerous for pups; appliances can be yanked from counters with disastrous results.

Look under your kitchen sink, and consider that a curious Beagle might get the cabinet door open. If you store oven cleaner, drain chemicals, and other household products there, install an infant-proof latch on the door, but be aware that the crafty Beagle pup may be able to open child-proof latches. Rather than chance disaster, temporarily place those products out of Rosy's reach. Laundry soap, bleach, dishwashing soap, silver cleaner, and other such products that usually aren't considered dangerous may present a serious hazard to Rosy. Other items found in average kitchens that should be kept out of your puppy's reach are plastic pot scrubbers, sponges, and steel wool, any of which can be chewed or swallowed and require surgical removal from Rosy's stomach.

Artificial and natural plants should be kept from Rosy's reach as well. Some natural plants are toxic to dogs. Silk plants are not only costly to lose but, if the tiny stem wires are swallowed, they can cause serious damage to Rosy's digestive system.

Though safe for your son, children's toys and treasures are a wonderland of attractive but dangerous objects for Rosy. Small foam rubber balls may be chewed up and swallowed. Marbles, jacks, wheels of trucks, Leggos, and Tinker Toys all may prove hazardous or even lethal to your Beagle pup. Usually, it's best to enforce an off-limits rule for Beagles in kid's rooms.

Window curtains and blinds are easily reached by an inventive Beagle. Books and expensive nicknacks are fair game for little Rosy. Table scarves may fall to her attack when you aren't watching, and tasseled throw rugs will interest her immensely.

Puppy-proofing Your Yard

Garages and garden sheds pose another set of puppy traps. Antifreeze, automobile chemicals, oils, greases, and cleaning agents are dangerous if stored within Rosy's range. Garden hoses make great chew toys; lawn chemicals and insecticides present extremely serious hazards to a snoopy pup. Even if the bottles are capped, Rosy might knock one over, break it, get the chemical on her feet, and lick it off. Don't allow her access to these areas until everything can be made secure and Beagle-safe.

Lawn and Pool

What have horticulture and swimming pools to do with beagling? If you service your pool, fertilize your lawn or flowers, or apply insecticides, Beagle-proofing the yard must be extended to include a few more points.

• Before Rosy is allowed in your yard, check the shed where you keep chemicals. Be sure it's securely locked, and double-check to assure that no fertilizers or insecticides have spilled on the lawn.

• When fertilizing your lawn, most product directions instruct you to water the chemicals into the ground. If you have done so, be sure no puddles remain on the sidewalks from which Rosy can drink.

• When applying insecticides, always follow the manufacturer's directions relative to the time that must lapse before allowing pets on the lawn.

• Never leave an empty insecticide bottle, pool chemical container, or fertilizer bag lying about. Rosy may sniff or chew the bag, or tip over a bottle, and contaminate her feet.

Next stop—the veterinary clinic.

After licking her feet, Rosy may become quite ill.

• Don't leave your insecticide sprayer out where Rosy can chew on the hose.

• Be certain Rosy can escape from your pool if she should accidentally find her way in. Pools are constructed for humans, not dogs, and the ladders that are furnished with some pools don't lend themselves to canine escape. If that's the case with your pool, build a wooden ramp and leave it in the pool when you aren't in the area.

A Few Answers

Invest in a portable dog pen to move from room to room within the house. Install infant gates to close off a safe room. If the safety of a room is in doubt and Rosy can't easily be kept from that room, crate or pen her when you can't watch her like a hawk.

Keep garage, workshop, and shed doors closed unless those areas have been puppy-proofed. Clean up all spills and wash the area thoroughly before Rosy is allowed access.

Introducing Family

Once she has become acquainted with her home, yard, and toilet area, you should introduce Rosy to your family.

Beagle pups are gregarious little family dogs. They rarely meet a stranger, and usually are more than willing to allow almost anyone to pet and make a fuss over them.

Licking is natural. Puppies lick the muzzles of their siblings, parents, and other dogs in their nest environment, where licking is the accepted method of greeting. Rosy is new to human society. In her human nest, licking is still Rosy's way of asking for acceptance into her new family or pack. Some human health authorities warn against allowing a puppy to lick her human family's faces and arms. However, this canine behavior is natural, and I've personally never known of any parasites or diseases to be transmitted in that manner.

Try this method to introduce Rosy to her family. Position the family members in a big circle, sitting on the floor or lawn. You carry her into the midst of this gathering, and sit with them, Rosy on your lap. Everyone is instructed not to call her, pat the floor, or otherwise try to entice her to come to them.

Release her from your grip. She will lick your hands, ears, and face immediately. Then she will frisk about and enjoy your attention and petting. However, soon she will become interested in another family member and will run to meet the child or adult, sharing her busy tongue with him or her. Each person may pet and speak to her when she is on that person's lap, but no one is allowed to prevent her from moving to the next person. In her own time, she will make the rounds and greet everyone in turn. She may return to you often, as if to get your approval of her actions, and she may show favoritism in bestowing her affections, but if everyone cooperates, this plan is sure to work.

Handling Your Beagle Puppy

Beagles are tough, hardy dogs. They are also rather small, and a Beagle puppy's bones are fragile and break with relative ease. If your family includes toddlers, watch both dog and child when they're together. It's important for small children to learn how to properly handle a tiny puppy, and that lesson should be well-supervised. Allow young children to hold Rosy only when they're sitting on the floor. Teach them to treat her gently and to respect her in much the same way as they learn to respect their parents or other children. It's okay for the children to pet her, but if Rosy wants to leave, don't allow a child to hold her against her will. Teach your youngster that Rosy isn't a stuffed toy and shouldn't be treated as one.

Encourage children to play gently with Rosy, and don't let the pup become the property of one child to the exclusion of others in the family. She may be injured when two or three kids are tussling over whose turn it is to hold her.

Children under the age of eight or ten shouldn't be allowed to feed the family Beagle except under an adult's supervision. Beagles usually are chowhounds that don't know their capacity. Children love to feed pups and have the idea that a dog should eat until she's full. That's rarely the case with Beagles. Vomiting and diarrhea often follow overeating episodes. To prevent problems and perhaps the expense of a trip to the veterinarian, take personal control of all feeding chores.

The same applies to treats. A youngster watches you give Rosy a treat to encourage some phase of schooling. You realize that the behavioral-reward treat is pea-sized. Using typical childish logic, the child decides if a little bite is okay, a handful is better, and the result is a stuffed Beagle pup.

Picking Up and Holding Your Beagle

Rosy's mother picked up her pups by the scruff, or loose skin of the neck. If she felt the need to carry her puppy from place to place, she held its entire head in her mouth. Those natural occurrences took place when the pup was quite small and light-weight.

Never lift Rosy by the scruff or forelegs, but rather, kneel down, slide one palm under her chest, and

Ear washing, Beagle style.

the other under her belly, and gather her up. Support her rear end with one hand and her forequarters with the other. Former President Johnson once was photographed lifting his Beagles by their ears; this technique definitely is frowned on.

Most tiny Beagle pups can be carried by an adult human in one hand. Slide your arm under her body, and support her chest with your hand. Rosy's weight is cradled on your forearm, and your fingers lightly grip her front legs. However, Beagles wriggle and twist, and it's best to use both hands or install a safety net at your waist. For the Beagle's protection, always insist that a child pick up and carry Rosy with both hands and cradle her in both arms, holding her snuggly to the child's body, taking care not to squeeze her too tightly.

When releasing her, the child should kneel and place Rosy gently on the floor. Children should never be allowed to drop her even a short distance. A fall of a foot can cause serious injuries to a Beagle pup.

Introducing Friends

Neighborhood kids can become acquainted with Rosy in the same way your family was. After initial introductions are made, Rosy can be allowed to frisk about and play with children of all ages when under adult supervision. Take care to prevent jealous or assertive possession by any child, and if the play becomes too rowdy, take Rosy into the house for a time-out period.

Warn all children not to allow her to mouth or chew on their arms, hands, or clothes. If Rosy insists, tell the children not to slap or scold her, but simply turn and walk away from her.

If play gets a little rough, and Rosy grabs a child's hand, that child should say "Ouch," begin crying, and with the hand hanging limp, slowly walk away, ignoring the pup. She will soon realize that biting isn't acceptable. Don't overlook the possibility that Rosy might snap at a child who pulls her tail or grabs her ear. Puppy teeth are needle-sharp and can inflict serious damage to a child's face or extremity. Even if the child isn't seriously hurt, your home insurance might be tested.

Other Dogs

If your family includes other dogs, introduce Rosy to them one at a time in a neutral territory, not in your home. The older dog should be put on a leash and kept under close con-

Puppies and kittens are usually good friends.

"Share my space with him? How humiliating!"

trol when Rosy is brought into its presence. Probably, she will act submissive, lick the older dog's muzzle, perhaps roll over on her back, and ask for the other dog's approval by whining. When the older dog has sniffed and pawed her, Rosy will hop around, place her forequarters on the ground, and try to interest the other dog in a game. She will repeat this performance each time they meet until she has been accepted.

One precaution: if the other dog acts jealous, heap praise and petting on both dogs each time they are brought together, giving equal attention to each. Be sure not to add fuel to an established flame of rivalry.

Other Pets

Remember, your Beagle puppy has many instincts of a hunting dog, one that looks upon rabbits, squirrels, birds, and other animals as quarry. It's illogical to turn a Beagle loose in the presence of a domestic bunny and not expect a chase to ensue.

Rosy is a trail hound and will love to meet your hamster, pet rabbit, kitten, or canary. Unfortunately, those small pets' lives might be at risk from the encounter. Rosy may accept these pets as friends if they are brought together carefully. Make it a rule never to leave Rosy with a small household pet unless they are separated by a strong cage or are closely supervised.

Cats are often great friends with Beagles, but when introducing Rosy to a cat of any age, remember to trim the feline's nails closely. It's possible she could be injured by an older cat's claws.

Bonding

The reciprocal process of building a trusting relationship between human and Beagle and becoming attached to one another is known as *bonding*. Bonding is a complex alliance, a learning process between both parties. A bond is a uniting force, a mutually binding covenant. Rosy won't understand what you mean if you speak to her of this procedure, but talking to her will increase the bond between you just the same. Bonding is more than trust, love, obedience, or confidence, although all these factors are part of the bonding process.

Puppy Bonding

When you first bring Rosy home, she's a frightened little puppy. Although an adventuresome Beagle, her human knowledge and experience has been limited to that which was incurred in her nest. She's only nine weeks old; how much can she know about humans and their lifestyles and rules? Her human handling while in the nest was important, but not nearly as important as that which she receives after leaving it.

You've removed her from the security and limitations of the only home she's ever known. This helpless little Beagle must be terrified by her prospects. The first thing she realizes when she's thrust into a strange new environment is that her mother is forever gone. Into this void, you must insert your friendship and love. You hold her, pet her, feed her, groom her, and make her comfortable. When she cries for her mother and siblings, you console her.

What is her response to this tender care you give her? She learns to love you naturally, but more than that, she depends on you. While you are gently caring for her as a matter of course, she's bonding with you more tightly. Soon, she will look to you not only for food and comfort, but also for playing, exercise, and virtually every enjoyable activity.

You call her name in a certain soft tone, and she comes to you as naturally as if she was always named Rosy. You reward her response with kind words and petting to show that she has responded properly. This is part of bonding. The strongest bond is the one between Rosy and the human who spends the most time with her. Because this person is probably the same individual who will housebreak her and teach her proper response to simple obedience commands, that training will come nearly as naturally as teaching her to eat from a bowl.

Rosy will form a bond of some degree with each member of her family who treats her kindly and to a lesser degree with your friends who visit. If she has no contact or repeatedly has bad experiences with a particular person, bonding doesn't occur.

Puppy bonding is a naturally occurring phenomenon in most instances. If you wish to strengthen that bond while Rosy is a puppy, call her name frequently. Each time she comes, pet and praise her in a quiet, soothing tone. What you say isn't half as important as your touch and voice modulation when you speak to her.

Never call her to scold or reprimand. Make an effort to increase Rosy's self-confidence and trust in you. Be consistent; each time she comes to you, whether you have called her or not, praise her and let her know she has done just what you wanted. Soon you will notice that she is focusing on you more and more, watching your actions and seeking your approval.

Adult Bonding

When a grown Beagle becomes part of your family, she too must be made to feel at home. If another family has raised Rosy and you obtained her from a pound or rescue shelter, you may get some idea how she was handled previously, or you may not have a clue. Bonding moves slower in adult-dog situations, but the basics are the same.

Patience is necessary and the most important rule is not to rush the bonding procedure. Be available but let Rosy become accustomed to her new home and family in her own time.

Changing Rosy's name has no value if she has come from a loving home with no adverse experiences. In such a case, using her former call name may reduce the stress of changing homes. However, the first step when adopting a rescued Beagle or one from a pound or shelter is to give her a name and use it often; a

new name will hopefully give your relationship a fresh start

Never yell; her hearing is superior to yours. Teach Rosy her name by offering her a special treat when she responds. Call her frequently to you by saying in a normal voice, "*Rosy, come,*" and reward her coming with food, not an entire meal but enough to keep her interest. Make the food treat something special, something she likes. This is easy with a Beagle; rarely will you find any food that Rosy doesn't like.

Feed her from your hand while you pet and praise her for recognizing her name and responding to your call. Keep a pocketful of dry dog food or treats. Her nose will tell her that you have something for her, but don't give her a treat until she responds to you in a positive way.

For instance, if you discover that she likes to fetch, toss a knotted piece of rope and, when she brings it straight to you, tell her, "*Rosy, give,*" and offer her the treat. She can't accept the treat without dropping the rope and she will thus learn another command without any particular strain on your relationship. Play tug-o-war with her if she enjoys that game, and when you have spent a few moments at it, tell her, "*Enough*" and reach in your pocket for a treat. If she stops tugging, releases the toy, and looks up at you expectantly, that's your cue to give her the treat. Soon, without effort and without realizing that you have been training her, she will respond to your commands.

Don't hurry to exert your influence on Rosy. If nothing of her past is known, allow her to move about without a collar or leash for a few days before you introduce her to a buckle collar. When she accepts the collar, try snapping on a leash and see what happens. If she has been taken for walks in the past, she will indicate her acceptance of the leash quickly and anxiously.

Experiment with various games, activities, and toys to discover which ones your adult Beagle knows and likes best. When you've discovered the activities she enjoys, ask her to play the games or perform the tasks she enjoys. Don't put Rosy into a situation where she is uncomfortable with you or what you ask of her. Try to make her believe that everything she does is correct. Ignore her obstinacy or stubbornness when it rears its ugly head, and concentrate on tasks she does willingly and well.

Above all, talk to Rosy. Second only to food, your gentle voice is the most important tool to use when bonding with a grown Beagle. If she consistently hears you speaking her name and giving her quiet verbal assurances, she will soon respond and seek your attention, the treat, and your approval.

Grown dogs must always be handled carefully, but that's doubly true when you have children. Unless your kids are old enough to understand the situation, it's probably best not to introduce the children right away. Be

A new pup will learn from an older pet.

sure the new Beagle is trustworthy, and let her acclimate to you and your home first, then move ahead with family introductions.

Beagle Socialization

Socialization is not the same as bonding or schooling, but it includes some of the same factors. Socialization is the degree to which Rosy conforms to your family lifestyle. It is her adaptation to the needs of her new pack, her human family. The word *social* has to do with people living together and sharing the same space. It is the way each individual acts toward the others and the effect each has on the lives of the others in the group.

Always treat Rosy with affection but instill in her that what you want is more important than what she wants. You are her pack leader and, one way or another, you will get your own way! A well-socialized Beagle is one that respects humans at all times. If Rosy happily meshes with her human companions and accepts her place in human society with dignity and a wagging tail, she is probably well-socialized.

You are an important factor in Rosy's socialization. If you make fair rules and insist on compliance by both dog and human members of the family, you won't find her socialization to be a problem. However, if any family member treats her arbitrarily and incorrectly, she may never become socialized.

A grown Beagle may already be socialized and require a minimal amount of your attention, but don't count on it. Make all rules fair, enforce them consistently, have patience, and display affection and you'll enjoy a well-socialized Beagle.

Identification

As soon as you've decided to keep Rosy and make her a permanent part of your family, she should be properly identified.

Tags

From a pet supply store or pet shop order a tag for her to wear on her collar. Tags are an important way to let everyone know your name, address, and phone number so she may be brought home if she wanders away. The problem with nametags is that your Beagle might slip her collar or lose her tag when running through brambles in hot pursuit of a squirrel. A nametag isn't a permanent, foolproof method of identification, but it will certainly help your neighbors know who is responsible for Rosy if she turns up in their yards.

Tattoo

A tattoo, placed in one of Rosy's ears or on her belly, is a permanent identification. Veterinarians and some grooming parlors do tattooing. Breeders often tattoo a litter designation, combined with a number. Your social security number may be

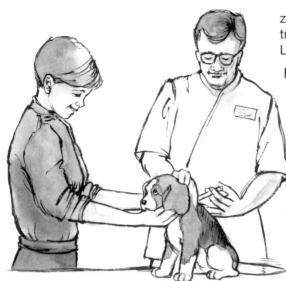

Use of an implanted microchip is a safe means of identification.

zation through which you can be traced. (See Useful Addresses and Literature, page 193.)

Microchip

Another means of permanently identifying Rosy is a subcutaneous (under the skin) or intramuscular (in the superficial muscle) microchip that will identify Rosy as your dog. This microchip constitutes relatively foolproof identification, but it is invisible and requires a special scanning instrument to read. Veterinarians and shelter personnel follow a standard procedure for placing the microchip and can usually locate the chip and read it in an instant. If Rosy is found and taken to a dog pound, animal shelter, or veterinary hospital as a stray, she will be scanned for microchip identification.

Because a microchip can't be seen visually, a tattoo should be used as well.

used if you aren't sensitive about this number being published. Rosy's registration number is great, or if your state has lifetime licensing, that number will work. The tattoo should then be registered with a national organi-

Chapter Six

Beagle Accommodations and Accouterments

Beagles are intelligent, caring, and clever pets, as we all know from reading the *Peanuts* comic strip. They are robust dogs, quite adaptable to both indoor and outdoor housing. Hopefully, Sam will be more conservative than Snoopy and won't require a typewriter, ball glove, or World War I flying helmet and goggles. However, certain other Beagle furniture and equipment are needed.

Outdoor Beagle

If you've obtained Sam for brace work or pack hunting activities or if for any reason you don't want the intimacy of sharing your bed and board with him, be sure he has suitable accommodations of his own.

Fenced Run

A dog run is a must for a pack of Beagles, serving to assure the pack's safety when you're not at home. A run will also be appreciated for a single dog to keep him out of harm's way when the yard gate is opened for any reason.

If you decide to build a run, construct it to last, using chain-link fencing stretched on steel posts set in concrete. It should be positioned at the rear of your yard in the shade of trees if possible. Make sure the run's height is sufficient to keep Sam contained even when the charming Dalmatian bitch down the street is in season.

The most practical run is 6-feet (2-m) tall, with the fence fabric extended a few inches into the ground. An adequate run size for a single dog is about 12-feet (6-m) long by at least 6-feet (3-m) wide. If Sam proves to be a fence climber, securing a chain-link top on the run will contain him.

The floor of the run should slope from front to back with a drop of several inches to keep rain puddles from forming in the front. The floor can be cement for easy cleaning but often it will promote elbow calluses and footpad abrasions. Fine sand is preferable because it's softer, feces can be picked up easily, urine soaks through, and the sand can be changed every few years if necessary.

A Beagle needs the security of a reliable fence.

Construct a wooden platform within the run on which to place Sam's doghouse. The platform should be set a few inches above the run floor, and should be at least twice the size of his house, so he can use it to lie on when the weather allows. A shade cover may be constructed over this veranda, which will provide relief from the sun and shelter from rain and snow.

Doghouse

Whether or not a run is deemed necessary, if Sam is to be an outside Beagle, he should have a doghouse. If more than one Beagle is to occupy this house, construct it to fit the number of occupants. If Sam is to be the only dog, buy or build a house that will be just large enough for him to stretch out when he is full-grown. Remember, in cold weather, his body heat must provide all his warmth, and the smaller the house, the less area must be heated.

A fiberglass igloo-type house is an excellent investment. It has no cracks to let in cold air, is easily cleaned and disinfected when necessary, and sheds water wonderfully. The short tunnel leading into the igloo tends to shelter the inside of the house from wind as well.

A 55-gallon drum makes a cozy Beagle house. This barrel is laid on a pair of parallel timbers to prevent it from rolling and to keep the barrel's wall a few inches above the ground. The open end is enclosed with a cover, into which a door is cut. A level floor of plywood is fitted inside the barrel, which leaves a few inches of dead air space insulation between the drum's wall and the wooden floor.

If you're handy with a hammer and saw and elect to build Sam's doghouse, construct it with a high threshold, one he must step over to enter the house. That will help protect him from drafts. The house should have no wasted space and should be only a few inches higher than an adult Beagle's head. Place the door toward one end so as to allow Sam to curl up without lying in the draft of an open doorway. In cold climates, fit the house with a plastic or canvas door flap to keep out cold breezes and prevent body heat from escaping. Or better yet, let Sam share your home.

Bedding

Beagles are tough hunting dogs, but they don't have an abundance of coat and certainly appreciate little creature comforts like warm bedding. Yard sales or thrift shops will supply a few old blankets for Sam's sleeping pallet. In damp weather, blankets can be rotated daily so he will always have a dry bed. Foam or straw bedding is difficult to clean and keep dry, often holding dampness for days once it becomes wet.

Indoor Beagle

Most one-Beagle families keep their pets in the house at night, especially in stormy weather. Beagles are clean dogs and if socialized properly, their manners should allow them free access to your home.

Bed

Sam's bed need be nothing more elaborate than a blanket or rug folded to his approximate size and tossed on the floor beside your bed. Or, if you have a flair for the elegant, it may be a fancy wicker, fiberglass, or wooden bed with his name

Your Beagle's bed need not be elaborate.

Beagle indoor housing can double as a traveling cage for car journeys.

embossed on the headboard. Rarely are Beagles taught to read, and, though sensitive, most really don't care if their sleeping place is thus identified.

If Sam is a wanderer and stomps about all over the house at night, he should be taught to sleep in a crate. Crating or penning is an integral aspect of housebreaking a Beagle, and if the process is introduced correctly, Sam will accept his crate with grace and appreciation. A crate may also be used to confine your Beagle buddy when his safety or sanity is at risk from rowdy neighborhood kids.

A strong fiberglass crate can be purchased at a pet supply store, and is available in a variety of shapes and sizes. Choose one that is adequately ventilated with openings on three sides and has a sturdy metal gate on the front. It should be of a size that allows a full-grown Beagle to stand upright, turn around, and stretch out.

If desired, a portable pen will serve much the same purpose. Pens usually are larger than crates, more difficult to move, and less secure for adult Beagles. They are handy to have when Sam is still a pup and needs restriction but afford less confinement than a crate.

Indoor-Outdoor Beagles

Regardless of his housing, Sam needs his own dishes and other personal items. Most of all, he needs the safety and security of a fenced yard. It's possible to get along without a fenced yard if you are really dedicated. Thousands of dogs, Beagles among them, are kept in high-rise apartments and are exercised in parks, on dog walks, and along street curbs. These dogs adapt to apartment living and are well adjusted and satisfied with their accommodations. They undoubtedly bring their owners great happiness and companionship. Who can argue with such a mutually gratifying lifestyle?

At the other end of the spectrum is a Beagle owner who lives on country acreage and allows his dog to run and play at will in nearby woods, pastures, and fields. It sounds like canine heaven, but free-running dogs are at risk when one considers livestock, wildlife, irate neighbors, ranchers with shotguns or rifles, and the ever-present auto traffic.

Somewhere in between those extremes is the majority of Beagle owners, those who live in cities, towns, and suburbs in houses, apartments, townhouses, and condominiums. For these we certainly recommend a good, tight yard fence.

Yard Fence

Being a very social animal, Sam needs the companionship of other dogs or people to maintain his contentment. Many Beagles stray or are lost, maimed, or killed outright because they are left at home alone behind what was thought to be a secure backyard fence. The problem is that no fence offers total security. Contagious diseases can be spread through fences, vicious people can toss poisoned food into the yard, and in the case of most fences, a Beagle can find a hole, dig out, or climb over.

A cute story came from Rose Arnold of Rose Run Beagles. Three small Beagle puppies, Clown, Candy, and Opey, managed to escape through the backyard fence. The puppies were spotted immediately, caught, returned to the yard, and watched through a window. Quick as lightning, they ran to the tiny, nearly invisible hole and once again squeezed through. After retrieving the pups again, Mr. Arnold barricaded the hole with a heavy wooden block. When the mischievous Beagles returned to the scene of the crime, they were unable to budge the blockade. Undaunted, Opey and the others ran to find their

Exploring off lead is fine after obedience is assured.

Weimaraner buddy, Rohey, and led him to the hole. The Weimaraner put his big gray paw on the block but couldn't move it either. With that the pups gave up, but not without first proving their ability to communicate and attempt to solve the problem in their own way.

One of the greatest mistakes made by a Beagle owner is to trust the pet's safety to a wooden picket or slat fence. If you're operating under similar delusions, you better think again about Beagle ownership. Many backyard fences are 3 to 4 feet (1 to 1.3 m) tall and should be adequate for confining any Beagle-sized dog, that is, if Sam doesn't pick up a scent he really wants to follow.

Once out of his yard, Sam is a stray. He may be quite sociable, but the big aggressive dog down the street might not wait for a formal introduction. Kids with air rifles may try to discipline the wandering Beagle, or worse, Sam may meet with an unseen car.

Some fences are made of chain-link fabric and the posts are set in concrete. The lawn is soft and cool; the yard provides sunshine, shade, and a place for Sam to exercise to his heart's content. Why should Sam want to escape? Boredom is the primary cause, and it will stimulate jumping, digging, or climbing. Beagles are inventive and clever creatures that will find a way out if they're left alone for extended periods.

Backyard living for your Beagle must be supplemented with play, training, and regular exercise trips outside the yard. If your existing backyard fence isn't quite as tight as you think necessary, consider constructing a run to confine Sam when it is necessary to leave him for a few hours.

Invisible Fence

The latest rage in dogdom is an electronic fence consisting of a transmitting wire that is buried a few inches deep around the perimeter of

"I don't know what this is for, but I love it!"

the yard. The confined dog wears a collar that is equipped with a receiver. As the dog approaches the underground wire, the collar emits a sound and, as the dog ventures closer to the buried wire, a shock is received. The electric impulse is sufficient to discourage some dogs from going further, but I wouldn't trust it to deter a Beagle that has spotted a cottontail scurrying in the distance.

Dishes

• Ceramic dishes are porous, breakable, and may be fired with lead glazes that can poison Sam's food or water.

• Glass dishes have the obvious breakage problem.

• Constant use of inexpensive plastic bowls may taint his drinking water with chemicals used in plastic formulas.

• Bored Beagles sometimes chew plastic and swallow pieces that may become lodged in their gastrointestinal tract.

• Most plastic is rather porous and will harbor bacteria if it's not regularly cleaned in a dishwasher.

• Stainless steel dishes are nearly indestructible, they will last for years, are easily cleaned, and are dishwasher safe. Invest in several stainless steel bowls for Sam.

When purchasing his stainless food and water bowls, buy a little rack that holds the bowls in place. This piece of equipment is especially handy if Sam is being fed outside because it can be fastened to the porch or to his doghouse platform,

Steel dishes are best, but full dishes are most appreciated.

thereby securing the bowls in one place. Beagles are notably vigorous eaters, and this rack will save you hours of searching for Sam's bowl after he has eaten.

Collars

Sam will eventually need two different types of collars, a buckle type and a training collar. The buckle type may be made of nylon web that is available in numerous widths and thicknesses and comes in every imaginable hue, including glow-in-the-dark orange. Some have a surface that reflects auto lights at night. Don't expect Sam to express a color preference; it's up to you to coordinate his ensemble or choose a color that catches your fancy. Buckle collars are also available in leather and

Teach your pup to respect his leash.

rolled leather. For a Beagle puppy, a flat, nylon ¾-inch (two-cm)-wide nylon web collar should be about right. As Sam grows, a wider collar will be more appropriate.

Training collars are sometimes called slip or choke collars. However, no choking is involved if this piece of equipment is used correctly. Training collars also are made from several different materials. Chain probably is the most common, but nylon or rolled leather training collars are available and will work similarly. Don't buy a training collar until Sam is several months old. At that time his schooling will be underway, and he will respond better to a training collar. (See Games, Avocations, and Careers, page 94.)

A head harness is a type of restraining device that is used extensively by some trainers. This rather unique halter buckles around the dog's muzzle and gives the handler good control of the dog's head. These devices are usually seen on large, aggressive dogs, and rarely would one serve any useful purpose on Sam.

Leashes

Leashes, like collars, are made of various materials. Chain leashes are a bit heavy for Beagles, and leather leashes seem to invite chewing. Nylon web leashes are available in every color, width, and thickness to match his collar. In the beginning, before Sam has advanced to obedience, tracking, or schooling, buy a lightweight web leash, about the same thickness and width as his first collar. Later, a stronger leash should be purchased, as well as a long, lightweight training leash to use in recall, fetch, and other schooling exercises. A spring-loaded, retractable leash is wonderful for taking Sam on a walk but shouldn't be introduced into his wardrobe until he has learned basic obedience commands.

Chapter Seven

A Tidy Beagle

When discussing grooming, we naturally think of coat care, but that's only the beginning. A tidy, well-groomed Beagle is one with a glossy coat, clear eyes, clean ears, and smoothly clipped nails.

Coat Care

Rosy's coat is close, hard, and of medium length. It requires very little care when compared with that of an Afghan or Poodle, but coat care is quite important and shouldn't be neglected. Trimming a Beagle coat is unnecessary, although in conformation shows scissors are sometimes used to eliminate wild and distracting hairs.

For most Beagles, coat-care equipment consists of a brush, slicker, or grooming mitt. Cleaning the coat several times weekly with a rubber currycomb or slicker brush usually suffices. Some Beagle owners prefer a grooming mitt that's worn on the hand, the palm of which is covered with soft plastic nubs. Short-bristle brushes have been used for years and work well. A chamois cloth, moistened with just a dab of alcohol, may be used to remove dust and dandruff and to put a glossy sheen on the show-dog coat.

Brush from front to back, in the same direction as Rosy's hair naturally lies. During seasonal shedding, more vigorous brushing will help to remove accumulated dead hair, and sometimes, reversing the direction of brushing will assist in dislodging loose hair.

Eyes

Rosy's eyes should be inspected every day and mucous removed with a moist cotton ball. If Rosy squints, her eyes should be examined closely. A tiny twig, insect, or grain of dust that's trapped under her eyelid could cause squinting, or it might be caused by a superficial scratch on her cornea. Persistent squinting, redness, or other abnormalities seen in the eyes or lids should initiate a trip to her veterinarian.

A Beagle is an energetic hunter that runs with her nose to the ground and her eyes wide open in brambles, brush, and all types of ground cover. After each excursion in weeds or woods, Rosy's eyes should be reinspected for the presence of weed seeds or other debris. If found, it should be flushed from the eye with tepid water squeezed from a saturated cotton ball. A tiny amount of petroleum jelly or mineral oil should carefully be dropped in the eye after clearing it of foreign material.

Don't use human eyewashes unless you are advised to do so by Rosy's veterinarian. Some ophthalmic solutions and ointments contain steroids, which might inhibit healing of corneal scratches.

Ears

Beagles inherited their long, soft hound ears from their ancestors, and these pendulant appendages are one of the charming qualities of the breed. Unfortunately, the length of a Beagle's ears may cause trouble. As a puppy, Rosy probably stepped on her ears when she ran about with nose to the ground. As an adult, she may find her long ears still in harm's way. Hounds often sustain ear-tip lacerations as they run through the briars, and to prevent this, Foxhound ears are often surgically shortened. In the past, Beagle ears may have been clipped for utility as well. No, we aren't about to suggest that Rosy schedule an ear job with the local plastic surgeon.

Grooming, however, includes careful inspection of Rosy's ears.

Nicks in the tips should be attended to when found. (See Ear Wounds, page 182.) Extend the ears upward and check the external ear canals for wax and foreign material such as foxtails and other grass awns. These objects should be cleaned with a cotton ball that has been moistened with rubbing alcohol or witch hazel. Excessive wax also needs to be wiped away, but don't stick your finger or a cotton swab into the ear canal. If a foreign body has made its way into the ear canal where it's out of sight, it could be forced deeper and possibly penetrate or injure the eardrum.

If Rosy whimpers when you inspect her ears, walks with her head tipped, or shakes her head excessively, look for dark wax in the ear canals. These are typical signs of ear mite infestation or foreign material lodged deep in the ear canals. These signs or pus and a foul odor from the ears means a trip is due to Rosy's veterinarian.

Teeth

At birth, Rosy had no teeth at all. Before you obtained her, she sprouted 28 deciduous or milk teeth. At about three months of age, these baby teeth begin to shed and are replaced with her 42 adult teeth. From that time on, weekly inspection of Rosy's teeth should be considered normal maintenance.

Retained baby teeth aren't as common in the Beagle as in toy breeds, but they do occur once in a while. In such cases, the adult teeth erupt through the gums behind the deciduous (baby) teeth, and for a time, Rosy will have a double row of teeth. This may occur in a single tooth or in many. When double teeth are noticed, pay particular attention to how loose the baby teeth are. If one wriggles easily, you probably can ignore it, and it will shed naturally in time. If the baby tooth happens to be a canine tooth (fang), which is solidly positioned behind the permanent tooth, it may warrant veterinary attention. Often, retained baby teeth have long roots; don't attempt to pull them yourself. Invariably, your pliers will slip off the extra tooth, fracturing it above the gum line.

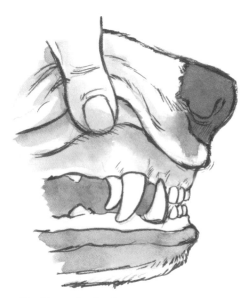

Double canine teeth may need veterinary attention.

Give Rosy nylon bones and other safe and tough chew toys to help her shed baby teeth and act as cleaning aids. Raw beef knucklebones may help cleaning as well. Be sure to remove all raw bones each evening; they can be sources of bacteria after having been wrestled around on the lawn all day.

Rawhide chew sticks, pig snouts, hooves, nylon bones, and similar products help keep Rosy's teeth clean, but rarely are they 100 percent effective. To assure a sparkling smile and sound dental health, you should personally clean Rosy's teeth regularly. In the past, hydrogen peroxide was used extensively for this purpose, but dogs resented the foaming and foul taste.

Pet supply shops, groomers, or Rosy's veterinarian can furnish canine toothpaste that has a more desirable flavor that won't be rejected. With a canine toothbrush, a piece of gauze wrapped tightly around your finger, or a finger-bootie, brush her teeth at least once weekly. Brushing garlic powder dissolved in warm water or broth is beneficial as well. Other canine oral hygiene products include washes, rinses, rope bones, and knobby chew toys, any or all of which may be of value.

Each grooming session should include inspecting for evidence of thick brown dental tartar and loose teeth. Plaque buildup promotes bacterial gingivitis (gum infection), which causes halitosis (bad breath) and tooth loosening; if either is discovered, consult with your veterinarian.

Nylon bones have many purposes.

Dental care becomes significantly more important as Rosy grows older. While in the prime of life, most Beagle teeth stay shiny white and need little attention, but as she ages and chews less, her dental health may deteriorate. To avert the need for professional cleaning or extractions, maintain a regular regime of teeth cleaning.

Toenails

Active adult Beagles that are exercised regularly may not require much nail care. However, puppies' nails usually grow rapidly and should be trimmed regularly. In either case, nail inspection should be made a part of Rosy's routine grooming procedures.

Trimming is long past due if you hear Rosy's toenails pecking as she walks across the room, or if they catch in the carpet.

Beagle nails have vessels and nerves that lie together and end in a pink V. Hold Rosy's foot securely in one hand and with a good-quality scissor-type nail trimmer, cut off the tip of a nail. Start with a white or colorless nail in which you can easily discern the V, where the vessels end. Don't attempt to trim the nail too close to these vessels, but allow a margin of safety as you cut. Darker nails present a problem because the V-shaped vascular network isn't visible within the nail. On these nails, start at the tip and make several thin cuts until the nail cuttings become softer and have cross-sections that are more circular.

Don't trim deeper than necessary! If you cut vessels and nerves, Rosy will yelp and jerk her foot, and the nail will bleed. A few drops of blood look like a quart when it's spread over a white carpet or tile floor. This blood loss isn't likely to be life threatening, but she will resent the pain that accompanies the act and you will probably have a tussle on your hands next time you reach for the nail trimmer. Always stop cutting when the nail no longer touches the floor as she walks.

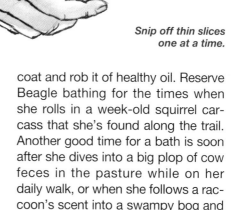

Snip off thin slices one at a time.

Don't panic when you trim a nail too short; trust me, you will. From your first-aid kit take the styptic stick, moisten the tip with a drop of water, and press it to the cut end of the bleeding nail.

A pinch of dry cornstarch or flour pressed to the bleeding nail usually will stop minor hemorrhage as well. Small, round, wooden applicator sticks that are coated with silver nitrate are expressly made to stop nail bleeding. They are available from veterinarians, pet supply stores, and some pharmacies. A trick used for years by groomers is to drag the bleeding nail across a dry bar of soap, digging it deeply into the soap.

After stopping the nail bleeding, put Rosy in her crate or pen for an hour to prevent a recurrence.

Bathing

Rosy doesn't need a bath every Saturday night like the rest of us. In fact, too much bathing will dry her coat and rob it of healthy oil. Reserve Beagle bathing for the times when she rolls in a week-old squirrel carcass that she's found along the trail. Another good time for a bath is soon after she dives into a big plop of cow feces in the pasture while on her daily walk, or when she follows a raccoon's scent into a swampy bog and emerges with foul-smelling mud up to her shoulders.

Another must-bathe time is when Rosy encounters a skunk. In this case, first soak her coat with tomato juice, let it stand for several minutes, rinse off, and repeat. Once the odor has subsided, bathe her with soap and water.

Unless otherwise needed, baths should be given about twice a year. Each spring and fall Rosy's coat will loosen and she will begin to shed. When this seasonal shedding is nearly over, and her coat looks a little dry and ratty, brush or comb out as much dead hair as possible, then apply the shampoo and water. Before beginning, place a drop of

"I give up. I'll just take a nap."

petroleum jelly or mineral oil in each eye, and tightly twist a cotton ball plug for each ear canal.

If you use your bathtub for Beagle baths, put a drain filter in place ahead of time. Run about 6 or 8 inches (15 to 20 cm) of warm water and place Rosy in the tub. Thoroughly wet her coat, then work up a lather with a good dog shampoo. Don't use an insecticide shampoo unless you are certain that she has fleas, ticks, or lice. With a hose attached to the warm water faucet, rinse Rosy's coat by holding the hose tightly against her body, minimizing splash. Repeat shampooing if necessary. Don't spray water in her face, and even if you've taken the precaution of placing petroleum jelly in her eyes, keep the soap away from her face.

Drying a Beagle is easily accomplished with a towel and, if you wish, she can be finished off with a hairdryer set on the coolest setting. Be advised that immediately after a bath, mischievous Beagles love to roll on the lawn, in the garden dirt, or any other place that offers scents other than soap.

Chapter Eight
The Active Beagle

Exercise

Exercise is essential for most creatures' good health and happiness. Until their dotage, Beagles thrive on regular exercise. Some sporting breeds, like pointers and setters, love to run full throttle. Sam's exercise requirement surpasses that of many dogs, but walking or trotting satisfies his need. Scenthounds like Beagles often are content with short bursts of energy followed by lengthy rest periods. This pattern fits most human preferences as well and is one reason that Beagles have been one of the top AKC breeds for many years.

If allowed, Sam will get his exercise following scent trails of other animals. He follows these tracks at a conservative trot with short bursts of speed when on a hot trail. He knows that running full tilt may cause him to overrun a track turn, in which case he will expend further energy backtracking to find the scent again.

Beagles have been bred to move at a moderate pace when working, so Sam will get his exercise the easy way. No matter that the frightened quarry was in overdrive, Sam's in no such hurry. He'd rather follow the rabbit's trail precisely than rush headlong, waste energy, and repeatedly backtrack.

Exercise Importance

In a conversation, if you were asked why you exercised, you would probably say, "I'd get fat if I didn't exercise." Likewise, a Beagle's exercise is related to body fat deposits and muscle development and tone, but it has a greater importance. Puppies need regular exercise to produce strong bones and joints. The mature Beagle's coat, feet, and body suppleness are enhanced by exercise. Exercise helps maintain an active, quick mind as well.

Your relationship with Sam is sweetened by the exercise you share. Regular walks stimulate conversations between two best friends. His body language speaks to you, and you'll respond verbally, assuring him that he's the best dog in the world and is fulfilling his destiny by walking with you.

The time spent exercising Sam is the foundation for bonding and schooling. Professional trainers emphasize the importance of focus.

"If my ears were longer, I could really fly!"

When you're walking with Sam and carrying on your conversation, he's constantly reminded to focus on you as well as the scents his nose tells him about. He'll concentrate on your words and actions until soon he'll seem to sense by your tone when you're correcting him and when you're offering congratulations. Although his nose will always be busy, he'll hear you tell him to leave this trail now, to change directions, or to patiently wait while you rest.

Playing

If allowed, Sam will track other animals without human leadership. In the company of other dogs, he'll show close cooperation with his pack mates in the absence of human friends. For these reasons, some behavioral experts have labeled hounds nonplaying dogs. They've reported that, unlike sporting breeds, hounds have little desire to carry objects and are, therefore, less fun to play with. Hounds are supposedly less attached to play objects, such as rubber bones, tug-o-war ropes, retriever dummies, and the like.

In reality, play has great importance throughout Sam's life. Frisbee, fetch, catch, or hide-and-seek are games he will enjoy, each of which affords him some active and useful exercise. Each new game brings another challenge for him, and a new way for you to enjoy your Beagle.

Begin playing when Sam first comes into your life and continue until he must be helped over the curb in his old age. The intensity of games tends to change as we grow older together, but playing is important for old Beagles as well as for pups.

Playing ball will give Sam some needed exercise, and this is advised whenever more extensive exercise can't be managed. Many Beagles are first-class fetchers and never tire of chasing a ball or retrieving dummy. Probably Sam will be equally interested in hide-and-seek and will surprise you by his adeptness at this sport. (See page 94 for a description of these games.)

Walks

Some exercise is possible indoors, but for a Beagle, exercising outdoors is almost as important as the calories burned.

While Sam is still a puppy, lay the groundwork for nature walks by taking Sam for a turn around your backyard. From that easy beginning, plan to spend an hour with him exploring the neighborhood. When he tells you he's bored with the route, tour a different locale.

If you have a park nearby, use it. Make regular trips to the woods, beach, or desert. A Beagle's true love is following daily replenished scent trails of a multitude of creatures. Sam will immediately tell you where other dogs have gone; his body language and quiet interest will tell you of livestock trails; his vocal excitement marks each new wildlife scent. You'll find the trip quite rewarding.

Soon you'll be communicating with each other at all times, and that, my friend, is what Beagle companions are all about. A half an hour of exercise twice daily should satisfy your health requirements and will probably give Sam his needed exercise as well.

Nighttime Excursions

If your work or school requires all your daylight hours, you still have weekends and evenings. If you live in a hot climate, you'll find exercise before the sun rises or after it sets is more comfortable than during the day anyway. Safety is a concern at these hours, but Sam will be on lead and his protection should be easily handled with a reflective collar and leash. Think twice before exercising your Beagle off lead, especially after dark. His nose will take him into places humanly unattainable. He may have run-ins with skunks, porcupines, and other wild animals, cars, or dognappers. In case you plan to exercise him off lead in subdued light, invest in a tiny flashlight that attaches to Sam's collar and flashes continuously. Another item that will allow you to follow or find him is a collar covered with tiny flashing red lights. The best plan is to keep him on a retractable lead that contains a flashlight built into the handle.

Automobiles and Bicycles

Apparently, some people's cars need more exercise than their drivers do. Don't run your Beagle beside a car. Many lazy owners attempt this practice, and often a well-intentioned run around the park ends in disaster. Running beside any vehicle, including a bike, may exercise his muscles, but does nothing for Sam's mind. Honking the horn or blowing a whistle develops no communication skills; neither you nor Sam will truly enjoy this type of exercise. If you can't take the time to properly exercise your Beagle, invest in a cat instead.

Jogging and Skateboarding

These activities can be adjusted to accommodate your Beagle companion, but they allow for virtually no meaningful conversation. You may shout, "Get out of the way" occasionally, and Sam may yip when your skateboard runs over his toe or passes too close, but that's about the most communication you can expect. Focusing on each other will occur, but only to assure that neither of you is injured.

Swimming

Most large dogs and many small breeds enjoy swimming. Beagles are not as enchanted with a swim as is a Chesapeake or a Spaniel, but many take to the water willingly. Swimming provides fine exercise for the dog, but unless you are a Tarzan type, the chance of mutual enjoyment is nil. If

Regular exercise is important regardless of the season.

Sam shows interest in entering a lake, fasten a long lead to his collar, toss his tennis ball in, and let him retrieve it. That's a lazy way to exercise your Beagle, but it may serve the purpose.

Before you begin your swimming adventures, make certain that the lake is not a wildlife refuge, and be sure there aren't submerged tin cans, bottles, or other hazards hiding under the surface that may cause harm to Sam.

Off-lead Adventures

For Beagle owners who live in suburbia or metropolises, it's probably never a good idea to give Sam the freedom he'd really enjoy. Typically, Beagles with obedience training still aren't trustworthy to release without a handle on them. Sam's nose exerts a strong pull on his mind, and his obedience training will be overcome by his scenting instincts. He'll be out of voice range before his focus on you is reestablished.

If you decide to exercise Sam off lead, work him on a line at least 30 or 40 feet (9 to 12 m) long in strange localities until you're positive he's listening for your commands at all times. Or better yet, why not locate the nearest field trial club, or contact other Beagle owners on the Internet and get involved with brace work or pack hunting.

Chapter Nine
Beagle Schooling

Rosy is one smart hound, but all the raw intelligence in the world doesn't take the place of education, experience, and sound judgment. Being bright is quite important, but that faculty alone doesn't impart good manners, obedience, focus, ability, or an obliging attitude. Intelligence is an inherited attribute that permits Rosy to learn by experience, example, and conditioning.

How many times have you heard someone remark, "Boy! That dog is smart!" Actually, the dog being praised may be of below-average intelligence, and the complimentary remark was aimed at a well-schooled dog that displayed a burning desire to please. The admired dog's attention was focused on her handler. She was excitedly yearning for the chance to display her canine experience and ability. Being smart is a start, but schooling is the key to owning a great dog!

Listen closely; can you hear reader undertones that sound like, "What's this guy saying? I know nothing about dog training!"

Sure you do. It will soon be apparent that we're writing about nothing magical or mysterious, simply logical progression from one point to the next. However, there are some important facts for a novice to remember.

Although various schooling is herein discussed in a stepwise manner, in application, it rarely takes on that cookbook simplicity. For instance, one of the earliest commands Rosy will learn is *come*. This is an obedience command, but one you'll undoubtedly teach long before obedience training begins. Leash training will occur at the same time she's being housebroken, and the various play sessions and games begin very early as well.

Learning is cumulative. It is the sum of all the knowledge Rosy will accumulate through experience, by watching other dogs, and by your conscious efforts.

According to British behavioral writers, hounds in general are often less biddable or less anxious to please their handlers than breeds of other groups. Hounds are considered free spirits that are less subservient to their owners.

Comments from breeders across the nation indicate that Beagles do have less need for reaffirmation of bonds with humans. Rosy will probably try to get you to worship the ground she walks on rather than the other way around. These independent-thinking little hounds often display less desire to instantly obey and are, therefore, less easily trained except by using food rewards for motivation. Fortunately, Beagles have great appetites!

The fact remains that a trusting relationship forms when a Beagle owner pays particular attention to bonding and early schooling. If you build Rosy's confidence in you, it is to you she will turn when in doubt about anything. Once she begins to focus on you and look to you for guidance, you're halfway home.

Beagles' natural retrieving instincts makes some obedience exercises easy to train.

Start Now

Begin Rosy's schooling the day you pick her up from the breeder. Puppy bonding is part of her first lesson, and you are her handler and teacher. It's never too early to start seeking her trust. Each time you pick her up for a cuddle, you're reinforcing this trust relationship and, at the same time, you're schooling her in the practice of acceptable behavior and manners.

That same day, you begin teaching her to respond to her name. You call "*Rosy!*" and she perks up and looks around. As soon as she begins to show recognition of her name, you add "*Come*" to her vocabulary. You drop to one knee, extend your hands, and she runs to you. When she arrives in your lap, whether or not you've called her, reward her with praise, affection, and sometimes a food treat. Let her know you want her to come to you anytime, not only when she's called.

When and if you decide to progress to formal training, it will be important for you or some other single handler to take control of practically every facet of schooling. This is because each person in the family has a little different approach, and if everyone is involved, the result will be prolonged, ineffective schooling. However, for the present, any adults in the family that can read and understand can act as Rosy's instructor. Try to coordinate everyone's efforts and make her instruction as uniform as possible.

This looks like a team sport.

Trainability and Intelligence

Trainability is an intangible quality; it's a measure of Rosy's desire to learn or her determination to please her owner and includes the manner in which she takes direction. This quality is associated with Rosy's personality, which is partly inherited and partly learned.

Once Rosy understands what you expect, her desire to please (and a few tidbits) will lead her to success. Your love for your Beagle will translate to consistency, treating her fairly all the time. She will thrive on this consistency.

Intelligence is a measure of the dog's instinctive problem-solving ability. In the best of all worlds, intelli-gence will be coupled with a highly trainable personality.

Schooling shouldn't be confusing. Practice giving commands; make them short, concise, and explicit. Keep your schooling sessions brief, begin teaching simple tasks, and don't confuse your beginning student with more exercises than Rosy is able to handle. As she compre-hends exactly what is required of her on one exercise, you can move ahead to another task, but return to the former exercise periodically; rep-etition tends to imprint the task more deeply in Rosy's mind.

Body Language

How do you know when Rosy understands what you are telling her to do? All dogs communicate with body language. If you concentrate on your Beagle's body posture and attitude, you'll learn what she's thinking. By her actions, her signals, you'll soon understand when she is processing your command in her mind and deciding how to do the task you've given her. Her response to your command is twofold. She will first signal understanding, then she will obey. Her facial expression, head position, tail carriage, and limb movement all have meanings.

Work-Play Balance

As Rosy's handler, you must understand that she can only be led to learn. As yet, we have no ability to gene-splice or transplant our ideas directly into our dogs' brains. Through patience, repetition, and rewards, she can be led. All your efforts to school Rosy will be defeated or at least prolonged if you bore or tire her with long training sessions. No more than a few minutes should be used on each exercise; repeat it two or three times, then take a play break. *Never* continuously repeat a task *until she gets it right!* That attitude on your part will be counterproductive.

When Rosy is still a puppy she has an extremely short attention span. She can't foretell what your goals are and doesn't think about how the stuff you're teaching will benefit her later. She wants to play now! If you insist, she will take time out for a lesson now and then if you don't insist on taking all day with it. If each schooling session is followed by a play period, both you and Rosy will be happier! If you both have the time and patience, when one schooling session and play period is completed, you can introduce another elementary lesson. For example, *come* and hide-and-seek exercises have totally different concepts, and she probably will enjoy both of them. If you want to continue working with Rosy, you can avert boredom by switching from one such exercise to another.

Commands and Rewards

What is the proper manner to give a command, and what type of reward are we talking about?

To *command* means to give an order, to arbitrarily exercise power over some subordinate entity. It's not a very nice word to use when schooling Rosy; command is haughty and militaristic. You might prefer to use *directing* or *instructing*, but when you consider what you are doing, *command* is an appropriate word.

When you give a command, you need not shout it or use a gruff tone of voice. Beagles have much better hearing than humans, and Rosy will be sensitive to your voice when it's at normal volume. Your command should be concise and explicit, with no room for inventive interpretation or negotiation.

Practice giving commands in a certain tone used for no other type of communication. Rosy should never have to decide whether or not you are giving her a command to *sit* when she hears the word spoken in conversation. This is one reason why we clearly pronounce Rosy's name as a part of each command.

When to Reward

A reward is anything Rosy likes, whether it's a pat on the head, a scratch behind the ear, a kind word, a special treat, or a bit of kibble from your hand.

Never reward Rosy for *trying*, or she will never get it right. Almost right is still wrong! When an exercise is not done correctly, simply change the subject. Don't scold or make a big issue of her failure; neither should you reward her. Instead, when she fails, pick up her leash and take her for a walk. Forget the lesson for a day and spend a few minutes with her doing an exercise she's already learned.

Think carefully about her repeated failures, and accept at least half the blame yourself. Are you giving appropriate rewards for her accomplishments? Consider her age and attainment; are you expecting too much from Rosy? Are your commands understandable for the age of your pupil? Consult with other Beagle owners and devise a better way to teach the lesson.

Value of Rewards

Owners often make the mistake of giving too many edible rewards. Beagles respond well to treats or tidbits of food, but those should be given sparingly. When a particular exercise is performed satisfactorily, Rosy is given a bite, just a little bite, not a handful of food. A treat should be a pea-sized piece of cooked liver or other yummy. When she is routinely performing a task, reward her sporadically, not every time she completes the task. If she openly anticipates the reward, it is probably being given too frequently, and if she's trying to get into your pocket, you know you're giving her too many treats. She must know you have control of the tidbits and will sometimes reward her performance, but she must learn that treats come when you say so, regardless of her opinion.

The second phase of a reward is your praise and petting. Some dogs will perform for this physical expression of your approval without any food reward. Although quite affectionate, Beagles seem to prefer a bite of food as well.

Treats

To be effective, treats should have a delectable smell and taste—a piece of freeze-dried liver, a packaged treat, or some tiny cubes of yesterday's roast beef. Little pieces of cheese are okay, but messy; the same is true of bits of hot dogs. Dry dog food kibbles will be accepted but not with the same enthusiasm. Keep the treats in a plastic bag in your pocket. The treat to be offered should be kept in the same hand that is giving the signal that accompanies your verbal command. When you see Rosy concentrating on your signal hand and listening for your command, you're getting closer.

Cheating

The first bit of philosophy when schooling Rosy is to make her think she's always right and never does anything wrong. This means cheating a bit. Let's say you walk out into the yard and she looks up, sees you, and begins to run toward you. Take advantage of this situation. Immediately call "*Rosy, come,*" and motion with your hand. When she reaches you, praise her and give her a dry kibble that is always in your pocket.

What has just happened? Without realizing what she's doing, Rosy is learning to concentrate on you and she's learning her name, the *come* command, and the hand signal that accompanies it—all those things, in addition to recognizing that she has your approval and a reward when she comes to you.

Each time Rosy looks at you, you've accomplished part of your goal, namely, her concentration or focus on her teacher. Take advantage of this focus. Each time she looks at you, give her the verbal command and hand signal to come. When she arrives, give her some other task to perform, such as sitting to be petted, then reward her.

Establish Rosy's dependency on you. Don't starve her, but schedule your training sessions shortly before her feeding times. Not only is a hungry Beagle more responsive to her handler, she is more apt to remember and appreciate the commands that led to the little bits of food. She will notice that it's always her best friend (and the alpha pack leader) who fills her pan, gives her fresh

If your Beagle lies down, immediately tell him "Down."

water, grooms her, and gives her pleasurable moments of petting and kind words. In short, she will begin to depend on you for everything enjoyable in her life.

Ignore Mistakes

Don't attach more importance to her mistakes than she does. When Rosy digs in the garden, chews the hose, defecates in front of the yard swing, or otherwise makes errors in manners, ignore them. If you hadn't left the garden hose out, she couldn't chew it. Accept your share of the responsibility for her error. Toss a chew toy for her, put the hose away, and ignore Rosy's inappropriate behavior.

Don't compound her mistake by calling her to you, then scolding her or shaking your finger in her face and telling her she's a bad dog. She won't know why you're so upset. She will always remember that she responded to your *come* command and was rewarded with verbal abuse.

Beagles are smart. If she irritated you by digging up the tomato vine in the garden, Rosy will remember how you responded. Next time you're working in the yard and Rosy wants your attention, she will begin to dig.

Talk to Rosy a lot, but don't anthropomorphize; Rosy is a fine hound, but she isn't human. Remember, you are speaking to a dog. This little Beagle is intelligent and has cognitive abilities, but she lacks complex, abstract-thinking capability. Converse with her, but keep your dialogue simple. Tell her things she can understand, even if no response is required on her part. If she's walking on lead being very good, reward her with an *"Attagirl, Rosy."* Watch her body language when you give her these words of encouragement. She'll toss you an appreciative glance or flick her ears, making it obvious she understands your approval.

Gentle Correction

When she misunderstands a command, make the correction softly; tell her in a conversational tone, *"Wrong,"* immediately followed by a demonstration of what action is correct. For example, let's say you're teaching her to sit. Give her the command *"Rosy, sit."* If she lies down, tell her quietly *"Wrong,"* raise her front end, and put her in a sitting position. Then repeat the command and reward her with praise and a tidbit when she performs correctly.

Experience

Puppies have discernment by weaning age and continue learning throughout life. By schooling continually, Rosy's experiences are broadened. More importantly, each experience expands her capacity to learn. In other words, her experience is multiplied and used in lessons that may or may not be connected with prior lessons.

For instance, in competitive obedience training, Rosy is taught to jump over a barrier. That exercise uses a flat, white wooden board that is held on edge between two posts. It's a part of the obedience trial setting. You first walked her over the barrier, which was a skinny board lying on edge on the ground. As she approached it, you told her to jump, and she stepped over the barrier. Then the board was doubled and doubled again. Each time she approached it she was told to jump and she responded, progressively jumping higher and higher. She understands your *jump* command and knows what her response should be because the command developed logically.

Later, in an entirely different agility setting she meets a tire or window-frame obstacle. They neither look nor feel like a flat, white wooden plank, but if you tell her "*Jump,*" she'll know immediately that you want her to get to the other side by leaping, and she may amaze you by jumping through the tire or window at your first command.

Illogical Commands

Never give Rosy a command that she is incapable of performing. A ridiculous example might best illustrate this. You lead Rosy to a 10-foot (3-m) solid wooden fence and give her the command "*Rosy, jump.*"

You're not only insulting this 15-inch Beagle's intelligence, you're giving her a foolish command she can't possibly perform. Such action will discourage an otherwise well-trained Beagle and may irrevocably undermine your teacher-student relationship. Similarly, commanding her to *heel* before demonstrating the meaning of the word will confuse and discourage her.

Fundamental obedience commands must seem ridiculous to a puppy. For instance, Rosy is nine weeks old, three days away from the nest, and you tell her "*Rosy, sit.*" Now where in her short life has she heard the word "*sit*"? You can define the word, explain it till you're blue in the face, and it won't mean a thing to her until you demonstrate the action that goes with the command.

Don't put Rosy into situations where arbitrary responses are possible, where she can easily disobey. For example, when she's still a puppy and is running free in the backyard, you give her the command "*Rosy, come.*" If she isn't on a long lead, she may begin to respond, then change her mind and decide to dawdle. She has independently decided to negotiate her response. She may come if you repeat yourself, but that defeats your plan. You find yourself in an untenable situation and resort to shouting, repeating the command, or allowing her disobedience.

Be sure you are always in a position to enforce each command you give with either a handle on Rosy or a treat she won't refuse. If you remember those simple ideas, schooling your Beagle will go much smoother.

Grown Dog

If Rosy is an adult when she comes to your home, the same general techniques are used as for schooling a puppy. Perhaps you won't be picking her up to cuddle as much, but when she shows slight response, follow the same directions as you would for a puppy.

Keep your new adult Beagle under constant observation or confinement until you have evaluated her intelligence and experience. If you want Rosy to sleep by your bed, put her in a crate within easy reach. If she cries, take her outside for a few minutes. If she panics when you crate her again, don't compound her anxiety by scolding. Confine her to a small room such as a tiled bathroom or a pen beside your bed. When you've had time to observe her habits under various conditions, allow her in more rooms of the house if her action warrants the trust.

For a week or ten days, concentrate on making friends with the adult Rosy. Reward her appropriate behavior with treats and ignore her unacceptable habits. Take time to pet and feed her from your hand, talk to her, and encourage her. Groom her briefly, and if she enjoys it, groom her every day. Your patience will be rewarded, and nagging will get you nowhere.

Mature Beagles should be accustomed to collars and leashes. Place a buckle collar on her and, if Rosy doesn't resent it, take hold of it when petting and grooming her. Snap on a leash and see if she has been taught leash manners.

Beagles several years old can learn new habits and new rules. The time it takes Rosy to respond will depend on your methods and the affection and patience with which you introduce the restrictions and schooling. Puppies have short attention spans, but well-adjusted adults will concentrate for longer periods before becoming bored. When you attain Rosy's confidence, she will yield to your gentle persuasion.

Adult Beagles may be slower to learn, but they never forget.

If you attempt to teach her something she resents or will not immediately perform, take her for a walk on her leash. Then, instead of starting with an exercise that you *think* she should be able to do, start with something you *know* she can do, such as fetch, come, or sit. When she performs the task correctly, lavish praise on her. Play catch with her, toss her Frisbee, or simply show her affection for coming to you. Eventually, reintroduce the problem exercise.

Schooling Methods

The methods discussed in this book have been recognized and used successfully for years, but they don't represent the only correct way to teach a Beagle. If one technique doesn't work for you, try another. Rosy won't grasp each new idea as quickly as you introduce it. She may demonstrate more capability in some areas than in others. If you see quick response to one task and slower response to other lessons, analyze your presentation of each before you criticize your Beagle.

Force

As you will see, in this book no single schooling method is advocated, but a mixture of techniques is used. Choose the ones that work best for you and your dog, but don't eliminate a procedure because of its name.

Force is a severe-sounding word you may encounter in dog books that has inconsistent meanings. It is a viable training method when properly understood and applied. In canine schooling, force may have nothing to do with discomfort, pain, or abuse. You alone can judge the value of properly applied force and decide if it has a place in your program. Whether or not you like the word, several elements of force are implemented in practically all schooling.

Restraint is a type of force. When you buckle in place Rosy's first collar, your are forcing her to wear a shackle; she certainly doesn't come to you and volunteer to put her neck in a restraint. When you snap on a leash, you are forcing her to follow you. When you picked up Rosy for the first time, you turned her on her back and rubbed her tummy and chest. This is a type of force.

Sit is said to be the most important obedience command you can teach your dog, because sitting on command is not instinctive for a dog. It's a learned behavior. By forcing Rosy to sit whether she wants to or not, you are causing her to do something beyond her instinctive habits.

Habituation

Learning can be accomplished by habituation, which means Rosy becomes desensitized or accustomed to a fearful situation. The disconcerting incident is repeated in her presence until her fear is overcome and she accepts the situation. You are actually compelling her to accept new circumstances through repeated exposure. It is the type of schooling

Dominance training is easy and fun. Start when your Beagle is a pup.

that is used to prepare your Beagle for some of the individual Canine Good Citizen tests (see page 105). It includes exposing Rosy to honking traffic and dashing supermarket baskets or people in wheelchairs.

Associative Learning

Associative learning is learning that relates an action to a reaction. In its simplest form, Rosy comes to you and you pet her. She does something you like, and immediately you react to it. She connects her action (running to you) to your reaction (petting).

The reverse is also associative and often is called extinction, because the habit may be extinguished by ignoring an unacceptable behavior. A preferred term is negative associative learning; it's a part of Rosy's human experiences as well. For example: She chews the garden hose; you don't scold her or make a big issue of her action, but instead ignore her, put up the hose, and walk away. She interprets your action as disapproval, and will soon understand that any inappropriate behavior will get her nothing from you—no affection and no attention.

Punishment

Punishment usually refers to your strong negative reaction to Rosy's action. It might be scolding, striking, or nagging your Beagle. Usually, punishment is the tool of the uninformed; it's the technique used by someone who doesn't understand dogs very well. It's used to dissuade pets from repeating an error, but it often compounds one mistake upon another.

Yelling or scolding can be a form of punishment or even abuse, especially when it accompanies a physical action. Punishment will probably be self-defeating because an unhappy Rosy will try her best to escape schooling sessions. She may turn a deaf ear to your commands, hide, drag her feet, or otherwise become uncooperative. Ultimately, she will run away and try to hide when she realizes you are preparing to instruct.

For instance, Rosy makes a mistake when told to heel, so the handler yanks her leash and the training collar snaps her neck. This is commonly referred to as "a jerk on both ends of the leash."

The next time she's given the same command, she'll remember the collar snap and think about her sore neck instead of the appropriate response to the command. Her hesitation causes a delay in response and brings about another jerk on the leash and a vocal reprimand from the handler. Soon the abused Beagle is overwhelmed and afraid to do anything when the command is given.

Remote Negative Reinforcement

This term refers to use of some device other than your hands or voice, such as a squirt gun. Water is quite effective when remotely used to discourage your Beagle from an inappropriate action. An example might be when Rosy jumps on the sofa the instant you leave the room, but jumps down when you enter again. By her action, it's obvious she knows she shouldn't be on the sofa. By directing a stream of water on her through the crack of a door, she will associate the unwelcome water with jumping on the furniture. (Distilled water is less likely to leave spots on your sofa.) Remembering this disagreeable experience, Rosy will certainly think twice before she jumps on the sofa again.

Use a squirt gun for remote reinforcement.

Dominance Schooling

Beagles aren't notably aggressive under normal circumstances and rarely display a domineering personality. Rosy probably won't benefit a great deal from dominance training, but the subject is so fundamental to dog schooling that it's difficult to omit from this book. It may be of particular value when dealing with a mature Beagle.

Pack instinct doesn't necessarily refer to a hunting pack. Pack instinct or pack mentality is the inherent behavior of all dogs, both wild and tame. Wolves and wild canines travel, hunt, and dwell in families, or packs. The alpha (number one) dog takes the leadership role in the pack. You can use Rosy's instinctive pack behavior to cement or reinforce your relationship with her.

With a grown Beagle, start out slowly. Try a few of the following procedures the first day. If you meet with little resistance, use more the next day. With young or mature dogs, keep each session short, no longer than five minutes.

Your objective in dominance training is to impress upon her that you are the boss, you will dictate how you will handle her and when she can go free. If you always treat her kindly and gently, she won't strenuously object. If she objects, take that as an indication that this training is needed.

Repeat this schooling every few days or more often if needed until she relaxes and accepts the procedure. Once she has accepted your physical manipulations and you have the dominant role in her pack, you can stop the frequent sessions and repeat only when indicated.

• Hold Rosy on your lap while sitting on the floor. Touch and gently massage her back, neck, ears, chest, and muzzle.
• When she grows tired of being held and begins to squirm, hold her for another minute. In a few seconds she will relax, and when she does, release her.
• Place her on a table and with one hand hold her muzzle gently but firmly closed for a minute.
• Open her lips and run your fingers over her teeth.
• Open her jaws and inspect her tongue and teeth.
• Stroke her tail, flex her legs, and manipulate each leg, repeatedly extending and flexing until she relaxes.
• Pick up and inspect each foot, spreading her toes. When she tries to draw the foot back, hold it firmly for a second before releasing.
• Cause Rosy to move when she is lying on the floor. If she has a favorite spot, move her and sit in that spot yourself.
• Always feed her after the human family members have eaten. Don't allow her to beg at the table!
• If you play tug-o-war with Rosy, be sure to win at least 60 percent of the time.
• Occasionally ignore her when you return home, and give her the anticipated attention a few minutes later.

"That must be my dinner."

• Don't let her sleep on your bed or living room furniture except when she has been specifically invited.

• Put her toys up out of her reach, reserving them for play sessions with you.

Convince other adult family members to participate in this "massage" and dominance training. If this schooling is carried out with love and patience, and never with a heavy hand, Rosy will accept her place in the pack and will rarely challenge you for dominance.

Housebreaking

Housebreaking is partly an instinctive behavior that is refined to meet human standards. Before weaning age, a puppy urinates and defecates without discretion, whenever and wherever the urge is felt. In this environment after weaning, Rosy might deposit her excretions a little further from the nesting box (den), but again, the elimination urge is met without regard for the location or type of floor covering.

That part is instinctive. The human aspect includes causing Rosy to think about what constitutes her den, and teaching her what is acceptable in human culture. This schooling will be accepted more quickly if your rules are consistent and enforced without punishment or reprimand for her mistakes.

You're now in charge and it's your job to watch her closely and respond to her signals. Your response to Rosy's bowel or bladder eliminations must occur within five seconds from the time she stops and squats. If you've missed this magic time period, clean up the mess and watch more closely thereafter.

Punishing Rosy will accomplish nothing! When she's performing a natural act, the reprimand will confuse her. Punishment includes scolding, swatting, rubbing her nose in the urine, and other actions meant to discourage her urinating on the floor. Within five seconds from the time urination or defecation is begun, it's already gone from Rosy's mind.

• Start housebreaking the minute Rosy arrives at your home. Set her down in the toilet area and slowly back off. At first she'll be confused, but if you repeatedly put her in this area, the odors of previous eliminations will stimulate her to urinate and defecate there again. After the first success, pet and praise her, making her aware that her response was exactly what you wanted.

• Watch for signs of elimination such as turning in circles and sniffing the floor, and get her to the designated toilet area of the yard before she starts or, if already started, before she finishes.

• Carry her to the toilet area immediately after each meal.

• When she cries at night take her to the toilet area.

• Upon her awakening in the morning, repeat the trip.

• After her nap, another trip to the toilet area is made.

• Feed Rosy at least two hours before your bedtime. Remove her sources of water after this meal, and immediately before bedtime again carry her to the same spot.

• Take her for a short walk before you retire for the night and end this excursion in the toilet area of the yard.

Until housebroken, Rosy's crate or pen should be used to house her for the night. In the absence of these pieces of canine furniture, she can be confined to a small, easily cleaned room. Put a chew toy in the crate or room with her and give her something

This pup should have been taken outside when he fussed.

with your scent to sleep on—an old sweater or an unwashed tee shirt will suffice. If (when) she objects to this perceived abandonment and whines, cries, or howls, you should carry her to the toilet area, put her down, but not play with her. She probably will look up at you as if you've lost your mind or, strangely enough, she may urinate or defecate. If she does, praise her and carry her back into the house and replace her in the crate. If she cries within a minute or two, ignore her, but if an hour has passed since you last heard from her, take her again to the toilet area. After waiting a few minutes, pick her up and return to the house, but don't praise or pet her unless she has urinated or defecated.

Once she has caught on to the routine, the housebreaking chores will disappear quickly.

Accidents happen! Sometimes you won't be there when she has squatted and piddled on the floor. Don't panic and, above all, don't make a scene. If she just finished, take her to the toilet area while you clean up the mess with an appropriate nonammonia type of enzymatic cleaner. Then deodorize the area with a commercial odor-masking chemical obtainable from a pet supply store. Remember that past urine odors stimulate future urination.

Paper Training

Paper training your Beagle is only a stopgap remedy for housebreaking. It can be accomplished but in the end is a duplication of work.

A portable pen or the floor of a small room is papered wall to wall with several thicknesses of black-and-white newspaper. (Beagles seem to prefer the sports section.) Put Rosy's bed in the room or pen and confine her there whenever you can't be with her. She will have no alternative but to defecate and urinate on the papers. After a few days, remove the papers from about half the room or pen and put her water dish and bed on the other half. She will undoubtedly use the papers for her toilet area. A week later, leave the pen gate or door open, but keep the newspapers in place. She should continue to return to the papered area to defecate and urinate.

Move the newspapers every few days to a place nearer the back door. Finally, position half the newspapers outside the door and half inside. A few days later, move them until only a corner remains in the house. When Rosy begins to beg to get outside to the newspapers, she will be housebroken.

Your next job is to get her to use a specific area of the yard as her toilet. That problem is another reason for not using paper-training in the first place.

Crate Training

This subject has been partially discussed in previous chapters but its importance warrants further exposure.

In her crate, Rosy will be safe from visiting dogs, children, or allergic friends. The crate serves as a den or place of refuge that should never be used as punishment.

It is nearly indispensable when housebreaking and will make Rosy a more welcome guest in motel rooms or friends' houses when you're traveling.

Give Rosy the command "*Kennel*" and put her in the crate with a fresh food-filled chewy, a nylon bone, and one of your old unlaundered tee shirts. Rosy should be praised when she enters the crate, but not when she leaves it.

After she is inside, quickly close the gate, tell her "*Wait*" and walk away. Ignore her pleas to follow. Return a few minutes after she has settled down, open the gate, but don't make a fuss over her. When confined for longer periods, let her out every few minutes, and don't ever crate her for more than a few hours at a time.

First Collar

Rosy should begin wearing a collar with her identification tag as soon as she comes to your home. It only takes a couple of days to teach her the proper wearing of this important accouterment. A lightweight nylon web collar is buckled around her neck, allowing enough space between her neck and the collar to slip in two fingers.

Rosy should wear her collar for several hours a day while you are

A crate being used as a den.

with her. When she's stopped scratching and worrying the collar, leave it on her all the time, except when she is confined to a crate or pen. The identification tag on the collar is worth your dog's life if she escapes from the yard. A Beagle pup will make friends with every neighborhood child, and you may never see her again if she isn't properly identified.

First Leash

After Rosy has become accustomed to wearing the collar, snap a short, lightweight leash into the ring, letting the leash drag behind her. Keep her confined to the yard where she is never out of your sight. Walk beside her, giving her a tidbit now and then while she's dragging the leash. When she no longer pays much attention to the leash, pick it up, keeping it slack as you walk along beside her. Encourage her to go with you by offering her an occasional tidbit from your fingers and give her lots of *"Attagirl's"* to keep her mind off the leash.

Repeat this exercise a couple of times daily for no more than five or ten minutes, then remove the leash. Within a few days, she will look forward to the leash, probably because of the rewards she earns by walking beside you.

At this point (usually about 12 weeks of age), she can be taken for walks outside the yard if she has been properly immunized. Be sure to ask Rosy's veterinarian if she is old enough and has had sufficient vaccinations to be exposed to neighborhood dogs.

When you are out walking, keep enough tension on her leash to let her know you have hold of it. It isn't necessary to yank or snap it, but let Rosy know you have control.

Commonsense Commands

Some of these commands have little place in an obedience ring, but make your walks with Rosy more enjoyable and may even save her life. Few books introduce these simple directions, and there are dozens of others, equally useful, that you may invent. Remember, Rosy is *your* dog and you should teach her anything that makes your relationship more rewarding. The words used here are common but they will vary according to the dog owners and the region of the country.

Come

We'll assume Rosy has learned her name, whether she is a pup or an adult. Repeated use and rewarding her response have accomplished that.

Rosy's first lesson is the *recall* or *come* command. This command has been mentioned previously, and her response should be nearly automatic within a day or two. In case it isn't, wait until she's across the yard from you. Then hold up her food bowl and

Heeling is unnecessary when going for a romp in the park.

call her name. The instant she begins to come toward you, tell her "*Rosy, come.*" When she arrives, excitedly praise her as you set her food down. She won't realize she has learned anything; her reaction to your command was almost instinctive.

If you're dealing with an older dog or if Rosy is a bit stubborn or doesn't respond to food (heaven forbid), fasten a long, lightweight nylon line to her collar. Allow her to wander away from you some distance. Drop to one knee and excitedly give the command "*Rosy (hesitation), come.*" If her response is slow or unenthusiastic, pull gently on the line, repeating the command. When Rosy reaches you, praise and pet her and give her a tasty tidbit, then release her from the command with an "*Okay.*"

Repeat this *recall* command frequently while she is on the long lead. When her response seems to be automatic, try her off leash, in the fenced yard. Repeat the command for every enjoyable event you can think of, grooming, feeding, going for a walk, playing, and especially for petting, but never call Rosy to you to scold or discipline. Each time she comes to you, whether or not you've called her, acknowledge and reward her response.

Steady

When walking with Rosy in an informal, Sunday stroll setting, you see a strange dog approaching in the distance. Your reaction should be to take in the slack in Rosy's leash, apply a little pressure on her collar to

By teaching your dog commonsense commands, you will have a more responsive, and, therefore, a more obedient pet.

remind her of your presence and that she is under your control, and tell her "*Steady*" in a calm voice.

When you first tell Rosy "*Steady,*" the word and your tone will mean nothing to her, but as she repeatedly encounters unsettling situations and you consistently calm and allay her anxiety with this word, she will begin to focus on you and listen for the magic word.

Steady is not exactly a command, but a word that is commonly used when tracking and the quarry is at hand or when entering a confusing situation of any kind. Rosy's appropriate response to "*Steady*" is to slow down, relax, and look to you for further direction. You should begin to see a change in her ear set and expression when she begins to understand the meaning of the word.

Whoa

This command is used when you wish to restrain your Beagle. When she's pulling hard on her leash because you forgot her training collar, in a calm voice tell her "*Rosy, whoa!*" and enforce the command with gentle, firm pressure on her lead. The response you are seeking is a slacking of her pace until she actually stops and waits for you to catch up. *Whoa* isn't an emergency stop, it doesn't foretell immediate danger, but it lets your dog know you want her to slow down, hesitate, and consider. It can be taught with treats, but usually they aren't necessary.

Stop or Halt

You're walking Rosy off lead in a vacant lot of an unimproved area of town. Suddenly, she sees a squirrel a block away, charges toward it, and at that same instant a car turns into her path on a collision course. You need a handle on her. She is running with throttle wide open for the squirrel and is near the edge of your verbal control. What do you do or say?

When you command her, "*Rosy, stop!*" her response should be to stop first, then try to decide why you want her to do so. This command is indispensable if you intend to walk her without benefit of a lead. Beagles have minds of their own, but this is one time you must penetrate into and beyond their independent nature and impose your will. Her immediate

response to this command can save her life.

Schooling makes use of a long, lightweight nylon line fastened to Rosy's nylon training collar. Introduce the command while walking on a quiet street. Let her take advantage of the long tether by trotting ahead of you. Then arbitrarily, in an excited, slightly raised voice, tell her "*Rosy, stop!*" At that instant, quickly take all the slack from the long line, and when she reaches the end, she will suffer a rather sudden gripping of the collar, stopping her forward motion. She will quickly step back when this happens, and the tightness of the collar will relax. At that point, you may want to add "*Rosy, sit!*" Or you may wish to simply catch up with her, give her a treat, tell her "*Good girl,*" and scratch her ears. Be sure to reward her stopping each time, and don't minimize the praise. This is a response you want her to remember.

Practice this exercise daily. Progress to new streets or walks in the park or woods, and practice the command in every conceivable setting. When Rosy listens for your sudden signal, she should stop instantly, look at you, and listen for your additional commands.

The risk taken when walking a Beagle off lead when not in a hunting or field trial setting is still significant, but this command should help.

Walk On

This, like *whoa*, is an equestrian command that many dogs are taught. The command tells Rosy it's time to move ahead. It can be used when she has stopped suddenly and the danger has passed, or it may be your suggestion to her to move ahead at a faster pace. Like the other commonsense commands, it has no specific uses, but is quite handy for both you and your Beagle.

It's easily taught by moving ahead and giving Rosy gentle encouragement with the leash. If you talk to your Beagle at every opportunity, she will learn in a few days what *walk on* means to you.

Settle

This is a nonspecific command used to tell Rosy to find a comfortable spot nearby and relax. It is used most often in the house when she is being a pest. Perhaps it's dinnertime, or she's bugging you for attention. Maybe a guest has arrived, she's greeted him, and keeps poking her busy nose into your lap while you and your friend are engaged in conversation.

Settle is a correction that means different things to different owners. The importance of the command is to convey to Rosy that she isn't being a bad dog and she isn't being disciplined, but her action is bordering on nuisance behavior.

This is an easy command to teach, especially when Rosy is still a puppy. You have a pen in which to confine her during housebreaking. Put a nice soft blanket in it, equip the

Begging at the table is a no-no, but this guy is getting away with it.

pen with a chewy, and when you next experience Rosy's nuisance behavior, tell her "*Rosy, settle!*" and place her in the pen. She may be bewildered at first, but won't see the act as punishment because she's furnished with all the comforts of home.

Then eliminate the pen, but be sure there is some comfortable place nearby where she can go, and tell her "*Rosy, settle,*" which you follow with the presentation of a chewy on her bed or blanket. Be sure the place in which she settles isn't far from you so she won't feel banished or punished.

Chapter Ten

Games, Avocations, and Careers

Beagles at Play

Your Beagle puppy is a bright, intelligent creature that loves to play games. His obsession with playing can be used to great advantage when it's made part of a learning game. Games may lead to other pastimes and vocations.

Common Scents Games

It's natural for Sam to follow your personal scent. You're always with him; therefore, his favorite track is always nearby. Soon he will become an expert in searching for and finding you. Your affection when he discovers you will encourage him to trail you again. His Beagle nose will identify each family member's scent and differentiate yours from the others. You can easily turn Sam's natural scenting gift into a fun, easy-to-play game to enforce his focus on you and the other players.

Wait until Sam is preoccupied with his dinner or a chew toy, then nonchalantly walk by him and proceed to a good hiding spot. Then softly call his name. At first, he may run about using his eyes and ears to seek you, but when he's unable to find you by use of those senses, he'll resort to his more acute olfactory sense. He will put his nose in the air or, better yet, to the ground, sniff, and in a few minutes, he'll be standing before you, looking for your approval.

Hide and Seek

As soon as he has displayed this propensity to seek you out, have a family member hold Sam while you walk by and proceed to some hiding spot. Instead of calling his name, instruct the holder to tell him *"Find Kit."* The holder releases him and, before long, he finds you. When this happens, make a grand show of affection, praise him for his accomplishment, and reward him with a little tidbit.

Next, you hold Sam while someone else runs by him into another room to hide. When Sam is released, command him to *"Find Chuck."* If he doesn't understand, have the hiding child softly call Sam's name once. That should bring immediate results. When Chuck is discovered, he praises the pup, awards a suitable treat, and is allowed to hold Sam while someone else hides.

Hiding places should become more difficult as Sam gets into the game, until eventually he searches the entire house and yard for a particular child.

Tracking an Object

Rub a wiener on Sam's rubber bone. One person holds Sam, the second person allows him to smell and mouth the rubber bone, telling him several times *"Bone Sam, bone."* The bone has previously been tied to a string several feet long. The helper drags the bone across the floor away from Sam and into the backyard. It is dragged across the grass and hidden behind a tree or shrub. You then release your Beagle, telling him *"Sam, find the bone."* Sam will probably follow the bone's trail, find it immediately, and return for another go. If he fails, shorten the track and simplify the hiding place until he's successful. Reward him generously for sniffing out the bone, but in case of failure, don't scold and don't reward.

Identity Games

Games you play with Sam while he's a puppy are learning experiences for both of you. When you hold his favorite nylon bone behind your back and ask him, "Where's your bone?," you're teaching him to

Tracking any living creature is the Beagle's happiest vocation.

identify that toy by name. Then hide the bone in some conspicuous place, such as under a rug or behind a door, where he can easily locate it by smell or sight. Progress to more secluded hiding places and, before long, when you tell him to find his bone, he'll be able to scent out the named toy in another room or in the yard.

To expand on this game, ask him to find his ball. Teach him to identify it in the same way you taught him the name of his bone. Hide the ball and tell him to find it. Repeat this until he always seeks the ball. When he has mastered finding the ball, and is confident in his accomplishment, toss in another task. Hide his bone in the same spot with his ball and tell him to find the ball. If he brings his bone, tell him "*No, ball.*"

This will probably confuse him at first, but if he learned the identity of the ball and bone well, he'll soon bring whichever object you ask for. When he brings the correct toy, the effort deserves a tasty reward.

Searching or Tracking Human Scent

This is another game that Sam should learn quickly because it involves finding a person by his scent. In this game, your friend takes

Sam to the edge of a field with a long, lightweight nylon line secured to his collar. You have entered the field prior to his arrival, moved a short distance upwind into the field, and remain hidden from view. Be sure you entered at the same place where the helper now holds Sam. The helper tells Sam to "*Find Kit.*" If Sam knows your name and has located you previously in other games, he'll make the connection. He certainly knows your scent, and should immediately begin his search. If he seems confused, your helper can bring out a personal clothing item of yours, perhaps a tee shirt that hasn't been washed. Once Sam has sniffed it and heard your name spoken several times, the search should be on. If he still

Getting acquainted, the right way.

doesn't get the idea, call his name softly.

It may take several tries for Sam to get the idea, but once he does, it will be his favorite game, even when you don't have treats for him.

Searching for a Friend

When Sam has played the searching game a dozen times, reverse roles with your helper. You hold Sam while the helper walks away and hides. Tell your Beagle to "*Find Joe.*" At first, Sam will be confused because he has become accustomed to looking for you, and you're standing right beside him. He'll soon catch on if you begin to follow Joe's track and encourage him to pick up the scent. If Joe has been your helper, Sam should already be quite familiar with Joe's scent and the game should progress without any problem. If Sam needs assistance, have Joe softly call his name; that should bring about results. From that beginning, you can teach Sam to search for and find any member of the family, whether he's following their trail or is given a clothing article to sniff and then search for the scent.

In these scent games, it's important for Sam always to succeed. If necessary, lead him to the object or person and give him the object to mouth, or let the hiding person give him ample praise and yummy treats. Encourage him to follow the trail, to find the bone, ball, or person, then reward him. We want to teach Sam that he will always win in these games; winning is paramount!

Catch

Beagles may or may not be good ball players. In case Sam is interested, this game is easily played and will offer Sam and you both some exercise. Kneel down in the backyard and get his attention by telling him "*Sam, catch.*" Toss a tennis ball directly to him in an upward arc, so he can either catch it or let it bounce and pick it up. Then the fun begins. Sam may tease by bringing it toward you, then running while you chase him, or he may catch the ball and take off around the house or behind a tree. Your job is to catch him, then tell him to "*Give*" as you offer him a food treat. When he opens his mouth to take the treat, take the ball and repeat the game. When the game is finished, put the ball up where he can't reach it. Never leave tennis balls lying around where they can be chewed.

Fetch

Most Beagles will enjoy fetching; some will begin as early as five or six weeks old. The game has built-in rewards because, each time the ball is returned to you, the game probably will continue. If the game hasn't much general interest for Sam, you should reward each completed fetch with a yummy treat. This game is different than catch because he must bring the toy directly to you each time.

The toy used here is a short piece of large-diameter cotton rope that has been tied in knots. An old worn-out sock or a small boat fender (or bumper) will work as well. A tennis ball or a ball with a rope handle are other good fetching toys. For this game, Sam should be wearing a collar with a long, lightweight nylon line attached. Hold Sam, wave the toy in front of him, toss it a few feet away, and tell him to *"Fetch."*

Sam will probably chase the toy, mouth it, then drop it. In that case, you take him to it, hold it before him, and tell him to *"Fetch"* again. Then place the toy in his mouth and lead him back to the starting place. Praise him, tell him *"Give,"* and offer him a tidbit. He can't accept the treat without dropping the toy. Add your approval with ample praise and repeat the exercise. As always, repeat the game no more than four or five times, then quit for the day and take it up again tomorrow. If he likes this game, it can be used in many variations. It's important to put away the rope between fetching sessions. Don't leave special toys lying about for him to chew.

If you wish, and if Sam shows a talent for retrieving, you can toss his nylon bone and tell him to *"Fetch the bone."* When he routinely returns the bone to you, repeat the exercise with the ball, always remembering to identify the object thrown by its name and, when he brings the toy, to reward him. After a few days, toss both the toys together, tell him to fetch the bone or ball, and reward him amply when he fetches the right object. When he brings the

wrong object, don't reward him, but ignore the object and repeat the *fetch* command.

Simple Avocations

Parlor tricks may be Sam's bag. If he's a ham and likes his treats, he should accept these games. If he shows no interest in doing tricks, don't dwell on them. After all, Sam is a scenthound, not a Poodle or terrier.

Roll Over

This simple trick is easily taught to many young Beagles. It requires a certain amount of trust on Sam's part, and you should be sure you have his confidence before you begin.

Kneel down and place Sam on his chest on the lawn before you. Place one of your hands, palm up, under his chest, between his elbows, holding his elbows between your fingers. Offer a particularly tasty treat in the other hand where he can see and smell it. With the treat hand, make a circular motion and at the same time, roll him gently over with the other hand as you tell him *"Over."* When he has executed the rollover, give the treat to him and praise and pet him, telling him what a good Beagle he is.

If the rollover upsets him, put this trick on hold until his confidence has grown a bit. As in other games, give him the treat only when he has successfully executed the trick. Never scold or wrestle him down; force shouldn't be used to achieve results, especially when the lesson is so immaterial.

If you wish to continue to try for success, repeatedly reinforce his trust by turning him on his back, rubbing his tummy, flexing his legs, and eventually, rolling him over while petting him.

If Sam is successful, repeat this trick several times daily until he rolls over on command without any physical help from you. Never forget the tasty reward!

Shake

Most affectionate Beagles teach their owners this parlor trick, but in case Sam isn't accustomed to offering his hand, you can encourage him to do so. Sit on a chair facing your sitting Beagle. Offer him your right hand in front of his right paw. Hold a delectable treat in your left hand slightly above the level of his eyes. The smell of this tasty morsel immediately in front of his face will encourage him to remain in a sitting position.

Tell him "*Shake,*" then reach with your right hand and lift his right paw. When the trick is executed, praise him and award the treat. Continue to hold his paw for a second, then let it drop. Repeat the exercise two or three times. Try it again tomorrow; you'll be amazed how quickly he catches on. Before you know it, he'll approach you several times daily with his paw extended, looking for a shake and a treat. If the behavior becomes a nuisance, remember who started it.

An added dimension to an old trick.

More Serious Diversions

With time, Sam will become bored with easy tricks and games and will enjoy more structured exercises.

Obedience

The AKC pamphlet on this subject states that obedience schooling serves several critically important functions. It strengthens the bond between dog and handler, increases your enjoyment of your companion, and provides for the safety and happiness of your dog. It teaches rules of conduct and affords Sam a type of instinctive pack order that is natural for all dogs. In so doing, it places you in a leadership role, which is necessary for amity and concord in the family environment. It aids in producing good companion dogs, which creates harmony in your neighborhood. If it can accomplish all that, obedience is certainly well worth your time!

Canine obedience is more than a competitive exhibition of your dog; it's a team project and is proof that you and he are partners. He can't earn a title without your help.

Formal obedience work begins with either a Sub-Novice or Novice level and progresses through a series of planes or levels including Companion Dog (CD), Companion Dog Excellent (CDX), Utility Dog (UD), Utility Dog Excellent, Tracking Dog (TD), and finally, the Obedience Trial Champion (OTCh).

Historically, Beagles aren't as famous as some of the other breeds in obedience work, but they can more than hold their own with proper schooling. In 1998, 26 Beagles earned their CD title, 7 earned CDX titles, 2 earned a UD, and 3 achieved TD titles.

Equipment

Obedience trials consist of a number of different exercises that vary according to the level that is being tried. Various props are used, such as broad and high jumps, and uniformity is critical in both the obstacles and in judging. These are described in the pamphlet obtainable from the AKC (see Useful Addresses and Literature, page 193).

Training collar: The first item to purchase for schooling is a training collar. It may be made of smooth, lightweight chain, nylon cord, or rolled leather. Often referred to as a slip collar, a choke collar, or a choke chain, this piece of equipment has a ring secured to each end, and when properly placed on your Beagle, and appropriately used, it doesn't choke. Sam's training collar should never be left on him when you aren't with him.

To form a collar from this length of chain or cord, drop the chain through one ring, so a nooselike loop is

Proper placement of a slip collar.

formed. The ring through which the chain runs is called the *dead ring* and the ring on the opposite end, onto which the leash is snapped, is called the *training ring*. The collar should be fitted properly, measuring approximately 2 inches (5.1 cm) longer than the circumference of his neck.

To function correctly, proper placement of the collar is critical. When facing the same direction as Sam, with your dog on your left, hold the collar so that the chain loop forms a 6. When you slip the loop over Sam's neck, the chain with the training ring (and leash attached) should be running upward on Sam's left side, and crossing from his left to his right over the top of his neck. In all obedience work, Sam is positioned on your left side, and when it is necessary to correct his action, the collar is tightened, then quickly released.

Leash: Being rather small dogs, Beagles' training leashes should be lightweight; ½ or ¾-inch (1–2-cm)-wide nylon web or leather leash about 4 feet (1.2 m) long should be adequate. The leash shouldn't be longer than necessary because a dangling end will distract Sam.

Schooling Basics

Informal obedience schooling should be started early in Sam's life and, in fact, has already gotten a head start when he learned the *recall* (*come*) command. Obedience is a community effort; it's about a dog

and his handler, not one or the other.

Keep in mind that most obedience commands are totally foreign to your Beagle. While it's true that wild dogs sometimes sit, stay, lie down, and so forth, these actions are never in response to a command. The actions are nautral, but their association with commands is brand new! Don't expect miracles.

Commands

An interesting memory story came from Rose Arnold about her Beagle, Ch. Chardon Run for the Roses. This dog was the initial Rose Run Beagles matron and earned her AKC championship at 14 months (with five major wins). She earned a CD title at two years. For the next eight years, she didn't compete in obedience trials, but at the age of ten, Rose asked and Chardon was able to remember the commands and perform the exercises flawlessly.

Beagles are bright creatures, and when Sam hears his name, combined with a sound (a particular word or *command*), he will learn to recognize that sound and associate it with a specific task to be performed. Rarely will he forget a command or the appropriate response once they are understood and filed away in his memory bank.

Keep your verbal commands to a single word: "*Sit*," "*Down*," "*Stay*," "*Come*," "*Heel*," "*Go*," "*Find*," "*Search*," "*Over*," "*Through*," ad infinitum. Novice teachers often make a serious mistake; they command the dog to "*Sit down*" or "*Lie*

Retrieving an obedience dumbell.

down" or "*Come here*." These multiple-word commands may confuse Sam and make schooling more difficult than need be. If you find yourself using more than one-word commands, reconsider, and if a single word will suffice, use it!

Usually, a command is made up of a hand signal and a spoken word that should be given simultaneously. Some dogs only listen to your voice, others tend to focus on your hand; the well-trained Beagle will do both! Remember to hold the treat reward clamped under the thumb of the hand you want Sam to focus on and signal with that hand every time. Each hand signal should be specifically related to the verbal command with which it is associated. Be sure your hand signals, like your verbal commands, are clear and distinct.

Don't repeat verbal commands; give your command once, in a short,

clear, and concise manner. Your *command voice* should be a quiet, crisp, conversational tone; shouting will only distract. Use a different tone from the eager, excited modulation that you use to praise Sam. Separate the command sequence into its component parts, which are:

1. Name. When you say "*Sam*," and hesitate, he should quickly look at you. When he is focused on your slightly raised hand, give the verbal command.

2. Command (including hand signal). Say and signal him to "*Come*."

3. Physical direction. Hesitate again for a few seconds, then enforce the command if necessary. Give a gentle tug on the long line fastened to his collar to indicate what action is required of him.

4. Release. Tell him "*Okay*." That release will let him know the exercise is over and he is free to move about.

5. Reward. This should include a treat, praise, and petting.

This same sequence of components is used in virtually every command. Occasionally the treat reward is omitted, and as he progresses, the physical direction shouldn't be necessary.

What do you do if Sam fails to perform? You certainly don't yell at him! The instant a mistake is made, tell him in a gentle voice, *"Wrong,"* make the correction, and start again. Never make a big fuss about his failure. Don't scold, lose your temper, or nag. If he fails a second and third time, quit the exercise and take him for a walk. Meanwhile, consider his mistake, the possible reasons for it, and rethink your schooling techniques. Maybe you're forgetting something or your command isn't sufficiently explicit. Perhaps you're progressing too fast and aren't giving him sufficient time to absorb and process your commands.

Before you start the exercise anew, run him through some tasks he obviously understands and performs well. Sometimes this tune-up will tell you what to do to reach your goal.

Sit: To teach Sam to sit, put him on your left, face in the same direction, then say *"Sam,"* hesitating before you give the command *"Sit."* A second later, when he's had time to process the command, give him physical direction by pushing downward over his pelvic area, which forces his bottom to the floor.

As an alternative, hold a treat in your right hand close to and above his eyes, so he must back up to follow it. He will probably instinctively sit down and tip his head backward to receive the morsel. The treat should not be given until he has remained sitting for a minute and is released from the task with *"Okay."*

This exercise should be repeated, with a short walk between repetitions. After five or ten minutes, take a play break, and return to the drill later in the day or tomorrow.

When one command is repeatedly performed successfully, proceed to another, but periodically return to each previously taught task to reinforce Sam's performance.

Stay: This task is usually slipped in with the previous command. Sam is in the sitting position, waiting for his treat. Instead of giving it to him, turn to face him, place your open right palm before his muzzle, fingers extended upward. Tell him *"Stay"* and back up a step. Before Sam has become totally confused by your actions, step toward him again, release him with an *"Okay,"* and give him praise and the tidbit.

Repeat this exercise several times, but not every time you command him to sit. When he no longer seems confused by your action, try backing up several paces, keeping hold of the end his leash, which is lying on the floor between you. Then return, release, and reward. When he becomes accustomed to this, place your end of the lead on the ground and back away 10 or 15 paces after you have signaled and stated the *stay* command.

If he starts to get up and follow you, tell him "*Wrong,*" return and replace him in the proper position, repeat the *stay* signal and verbal command, and back away again, but for a shorter distance.

Sam's concentration and trust in your return is important to this exercise. As you proceed to the next step, you'll be out of Sam's sight. Be sure you don't leave his field of vision too long in the beginning. Each time you lengthen the time away from him, you should make your praise and excitement more emphatic when you return. If he is thinking about the reward, his concentration is less likely to shift to another dog or someone else in the vicinity.

Down: One of the most useful obedience commands can be used in many instances. *Down* is sometimes used after *sit*, but it doesn't necessarily follow that command. It's a separate command that requires another specific action from Sam. It can be used alone to put him in a lying or *down* position when you stop while on a walk.

The command is "*Sam* (hesitation), *down*." Enforce the command with gentle pressure on Sam's back to push his belly to the floor.

Another method of teaching this command is to hold the tidbit in your

Heel being judged in obedience trial.

right hand, on the floor between his forefeet. He should drop to his chest to reach the treat.

Another technique is to put him first in the *sit* position, then, following his response to *sit*, fold his elbows, placing his belly against the floor. Don't always follow *sit* with *down*, or he will get the impression *sit* and *down* are always used together, resulting in poor performance of either task separately.

Allow him to stay in the *down* position for several seconds, release with an "*Okay*," and reward him. When Sam is comfortably responding to this command, progress to the next step, which is a repeat of the *stay* exercise combined with *down*.

Heel: This task is probably more foreign to canine nature than any other obedience exercise. When you think of it, why should Sam always walk on your left, with his muzzle even with your leg? How could dog's best friend devise an exercise so rigid and unyielding?

However, *heel* should be taught to every dog, if for no other reason than it is a control exercise. Because this task is so inflexible, after it's mastered, it should be demanded of your Beagle only periodically and when necessary for his safety, such as when walking in a crowd or when actually practicing or performing in an obedience ring.

The exercise is begun with Sam sitting on your left, facing in the same direction. Hold his lead in your right hand and let it run through your left hand for control. As you step off with your left foot, give the command "*Heel.*"

He won't have a clue about what you mean and will try to cross in front of you or behind you. He might hesitate or try to forge ahead. Your job is to control him with the lead and your voice, to keep his nose even with your thigh. Use only gentle pressure on the training collar; never jerk it or try to subdue him with upward pressure on the lead. Without yanking, tighten, then loosen the leash as he correctly responds.

Talk to Sam; that's what he understands. Tell him "*Good boy*" when he's attained the correct position, "*Steady*" when he tries to move ahead of your thigh, and "*Walk on*" when he lags behind. Walk with him at heel for a couple of minutes, then stop, tell him to sit, release him, and reward a job well done.

This task is difficult for Sam to comprehend, but he'll catch on if you persist and encourage him. Spend no more than a few minutes each training session, but repeat the exercise regularly for short periods.

Canine Good Citizen (CGC) Test

With a bit of refinement, this AKC-recognized title can be won by every Beagle that is well-schooled in good manners. The test is an evaluation with a passing or failing score; there is no competition between dogs. The officers of an AKC-approved dog club will administer and evaluate Sam's performance, and if he passes, he will be awarded a certificate. Sam should be finished with his good-manners schooling and should know some simple obedience commands before starting this project. The CGC title is an excellent basis for a therapy dog.

The CGC test involves ten different tasks, each of which you can teach Sam without professional help. Here again, you can take advantage of classes that are given by dog clubs if you prefer. The basic exercises of this event are listed below. CGC is a very worthwhile project, and if you're interested in schooling Sam, you can learn more about this title by contacting the AKC (see Useful Addresses and Literature, page 193).

(1) Accepting a Friendly Stranger

In this exercise, your control of Sam is evaluated when a friendly person is met on the street or in your home. Your Beagle is expected to allow the person to approach without barking or growling. This drill should be easy for Sam.

The evaluator walks up to you and Sam, stops, talks, and shakes hands with you, paying no attention to Sam. Sam passes the test if he keeps his position without retreating behind you and shows no fear of or aggression toward the evaluator.

Performance requires Sam to be comfortable with strangers, which should be a snap for any Beagle. You can teach him to remain quiet by standing on his leash while he sits or stands at your side.

Friends whom Sam hasn't met can be employed to approach you and Sam one at a time while you stand beside him. When each one nears your position, reassure Sam with some quieting words, stand on his leash to hold him in place, and greet the person. Each stranger greets you, shakes your hand, and converses with you for a few seconds, then moves on. Don't forget Sam's treat each time he has remained calmly in place.

(2) Sitting Politely for Petting

This exercise is difficult for affectionate Beagles; they usually want to add some wriggling and licking to the perfomance. The exercise is meant to demonstrate the behavior of a trusting dog, but for most Beagles, it's more an exercise of controlled affection. If Sam has mastered some obedience commands, you can tell him to sit and stay. If not, you can again step on his leash after you've placed him in the sitting position. Once Sam is sitting, the evaluator will approach, pet his head and body, and circle your Beagle and you. During the evaluator's handling, you can talk to Sam, assuring your approval. To earn a passing mark, Sam must passively allow the evaluator's petting while in the sitting position, and show no timidity or aggressiveness.

Once again, the important part of training is to try to keep Sam's focus on *you* and not on the evaluator. If he's looking at you, watching your hands, listening to your voice, he will have no trouble with this exercise. Easier said than done with a demonstrative Beagle? Yes, but with determination it can be accomplished.

(3) Appearance and Grooming

Sam's overall condition is first visually inspected by the evaluator, who will then lightly brush him and physically pick up each foot and look at his ears. During this inspection, you can verbally speak to Sam, reassuring him that all is well.

Ask family members and friends to participate in schooling. Sam soon will become accustomed to this grooming attention by anyone while you are present and give approval. Don't forget, the key to this test is the *stranger*. Sam must trust you, and you must reassure him that the person is okay.

(4) Out for a Walk

This exercise isn't the same as heeling, but you can keep Sam at heel if he is already trained to this command. This CGC exercise is to show that you have leash control of your Beagle, but he can be walking on your right side. The evaluator will give you instructions to turn each way, reverse your direction, and stop. As in the other tests, verbally reassuring your dog is encouraged.

(5) Walking Through a Crowd

This exercise is another that's more difficult because of the typical

Sitting off lead with intense focus on the handler.

personality of the Beagle. Sam is required to walk on lead with you through a group of people and their dogs in a public place. To receive a passing mark, he must display no more than natural interest in the dogs or their masters, and show no aggressiveness or shyness toward either.

Sam will fail if he tugs at the leash or tries to play with the other dogs. Here again, the key to success is his focus on you. Talk him through this exercise, and be sure to praise him when he receives the evaluator's nod.

Schooling for this task is best done by first taking him on controlled walks on the quietest streets of town.

Gradually progress to more populated streets, always trying to keep his concentration on you and your voice. Signal him with the leash when you are about to meet a strange dog, and if needed, use a treat to regain his focus if it seems to be slipping away.

(6) Sit and Down on Command/Staying in Place

This part of the CGC test has several phases that will be easier if Sam has mastered some obedience commands. First, you give him the *sit* and *down* commands, followed by the *stay* command. Then you walk away, never letting go of his 20-foot (6-m) lead.

Gentle hand or leash pressure may be used to position him when the evaluator tells you to begin, but many evaluators will encourage you not to touch him, and treats can't be used to get him into position. When the evaluator tells you to leave your dog, you walk the length of the lead and Sam must stay in place, but may change positions. You are then told to return to your dog, take your former position beside him, and release him from the *stay*.

(7) Coming When Called

Recall, initiated by the *come* command, is almost the first task Sam learned. In this test, you first position your Beagle at a given point, tell him to *stay* or *wait*, and walk 10 feet (3 m) away. You turn to face Sam and, when the evaluator signals you, you call him to you with the familiar *come* command.

(8) Reaction to Another Dog

This is another test that is easier taught to dogs with less social affability than the Beagle. This exercise is a bit tougher for puppies and is a real test of their ability to focus on their handler. With Sam on lead, you walk down the sidewalk. You meet a stranger who also has a polite, well-behaved dog on a leash. You meet, stop, speak, shake hands, and continue on your respective ways. Sam's part in this exercise is to show no more than casual interest in the stranger or the other dog. If the participants keep their dogs on their left sides, the whole exercise goes smoother, and if you have taught Sam to sit when you stop, it should be a snap.

Schooling requires that you enlist the aid of friends who have dogs with whom Sam isn't acquainted.

First, pass the stranger and dog without stopping or hesitating. Maintain Sam's concentration on you and divert his attention from the other dog by constantly talking to him. Keep Sam's lead snug, controlling his actions. As you pass, speak to your friend in passing.

Reward your Beagle with a tasty treat if he gave the dog only perfunctory attention; give no reward if he tugged at the leash.

Repeat this process until Sam passes dogs without a second thought, then introduce the second phase. Stop and talk with the stranger for a few seconds, shake hands, and continue your walk. If you put Sam in a *sit-stay* position when you stop, and step on his leash, you'll achieve quicker success.

(9) Reacting to Distractions

Several sound and motion distractions are commonly used in this test. The evaluator causes a noise distraction, such as the slamming or sudden opening of a nearby door. Another noise that is sometimes used is the sound of a book being dropped flat on the floor, about 10 or 12 feet (3–3.5 m) behind Sam. Occasionally, the evaluator may knock over a chair 6 or 8 feet (2 or 3 m) from Sam or ask you to pass people who are engaged in loud talk and backslapping about 10 feet (3 m) from Sam.

Another part of the test is a visual distraction. It may be a person on a bicycle who rides about 6 feet (2 m) from your dog or someone pushing a rattling grocery cart passing about 10 feet (3 m) from Sam. Other motion distractions might be someone running across your path, or crossing your path on crutches, in a wheelchair, or using a walker.

Sam is expected to watch these events with natural curiosity, but he shouldn't try to escape from them, bark, or show any fear of them.

To school your Beagle, condition him by repeated exposure to similar distractions. Take him to areas where whistles, horns, and noises are common, such as in downtown business districts. Maintain him on a close lead, talking to him constantly. Keep his concentration on your voice and body.

The visual distractions are handled by taking him into supermarket parking lots and busy streets. If your Beagle is quiet and trustworthy, contact a nursing home administrator in your area and ask if you and Sam can visit. Once inside, he'll discover crutches, wheelchairs, canes, and walkers, which may initially surprise him. He should look beyond these appliances to enjoy his association with elderly people. Both his CGC title and his Therapy Dog certification will allow him to make a significant contribution to residents who see few dogs in their midst and appreciate the chance to pet a well-behaved Beagle.

(10) Supervised Separation

This exercise isn't difficult for most Beagles. Sam is placed on a 6-foot (2-m) lead, which is handed to the evaluator while you leave the area for three minutes.

He passes the test if he remains calmly with the evaluator without barking, pacing, whining, or tugging the lead. He needn't hold a particular position, and can move about as long as he doesn't become terribly agitated while you're away.

Schooling consists of repeatedly leaving Sam tied for a few minutes. When you leave, give him the *wait* command. Start with an absence of 30 seconds, then a minute, two minutes, and so on. Rewards are very important; heap your praise on him and give him tasty treats each time you rejoin him, but try not to get him excited at your arrival, or he will blow the entire program with his anxiety.

Formal Obedience Training

If you want to continue Sam's schooling in obedience work and perhaps enter him in competition, you should contact a local dog club. Only by training with other people and their dogs can you attain any appreciable efficiency in an AKC Obedience ring.

Earning a CD title is rewarding and progression to more advanced titles is exhilarating! Contact the AKC for the names of the closest all-breed or obedience training clubs. First, watch a class without Sam. Talk with the instructors and participants and make up your mind if obedience work is for you and Sam.

Agility

Agility is fun for participants and spectators alike, and if you have an active agility club in your area, attend a trial. First held in England in 1978, agility trials came to the United States in the early 1980s. In 1986, the United States Dog Agility Association (USDAA) was founded, using the British format and course obstacles. The USDAA began awarding Agility titles earned in trials held under their supervision in 1990. Agility Dog (AD), Advanced Agility Dog (AAD), and Master Agility Dog (MAD) titles are earned and may be suffixed to your Beagle's registered name.

Agility promotes conditioning, focus of dogs on their handlers, and

Agility jump is taken in stride.

a great camaraderie between competitors and their dogs. Here is a sport that requires no structured training, one that is sure to appeal to bored dogs and their equally bored owners. Contestants are free to work the course at their own pace (as directed and within time-limit constraints). Points are deducted from Sam's speed score for each obstacle he fails to complete within the course.

Sometimes, trainers have found agility training to be a means of correcting attention and focus problems in other activities. Dogs seem to appreciate the freedom to express themselves and to ham it up, working for audience and handler appreciation (and treats).

To participate successfully in this sport, Sam must be in top nutritional condition, physically sound, trainable, and intelligent. He won't be penalized for his faults of conformation or size or for being neutered. Naturally, because dogs are worked off leash, Sam must have a biddable temperament and amicable personality. Some obedience training is necessary before he is worked off lead in the same arena as other dogs.

Agility Trials

AKC Agility Trials are divided into basic levels and more advanced competition. To enter, dogs must be at least one year old and registered with the AKC. Spayed bitches and neutered males are eligible but lame dogs or those wearing bandages are not allowed to enter. Oversized Beagles are considered equally with AKC Champions.

Title and Awards

The AKC titles earned are Novice Agility (NA), Open Agility (OA), Agility Excellent (AX), and Master Agility Excellent (MX).

In order for Sam to earn these titles, he must acquire qualifying scores in three separate trials under two different judges. One title must be earned before the next level of competition is attempted. The MX title is earned after a dog has been awarded the AX title and has received qualifying scores in ten separate trials. When earned, the title abbreviation is suffixed to Sam's registered name.

Necessary Schooling

Schooling is accomplished with the use of a snug, web buckle collar, and a short, lightweight leash. Some tasty morsel inducements are necessary for most Beagles as well. Often, handlers will keep a small plastic bag filled with rewards in their signal hand to maintain Sam's concentration on that hand.

As you would expect, Beagles that have learned the *recall* or *come* command well often progress in agility quite smoothly. When teaching, the same principles apply as in other lessons. Give your hand signal and verbal command simultaneously so Sam will not focus on your hand signals exclusively, but will listen to what you say as well.

There are no official commands for agility work; any single-or two-word direction is okay. Sam will identify the words with the desired actions and with the hand signals. Plainly point your open hand and fingers at the obstacle and command Sam to "*Take it,*" "*Jump,*" "*Over,*" or "*Through.*"

Give the hand signal in the same manner that voice commands are given: distinctly, consistently, and without flourishes. Don't shout your verbal commands, but allow your excitement to accompany each hand signal and your voice.

As in other training, don't negotiate a command with Sam. Once given, a command must be obeyed before the expected treat is awarded.

Agility Equipment

Contact the AKC for a copy of *Regulations for Agility Trials.* In this little blue booklet are described the various obstacles, and from those descriptions and pictures, most equipment can be easily constructed by someone who is handy with tools.

Contact obstacles include the dog walk, A-frame, crossover, and seesaw. They are so named because the ends of each obstacle are painted a contrasting color and, in order to score in a trial, Sam must touch or contact the painted surface with at least one paw as he jumps onto and off the obstacle.

Agility trials use many other props and obstacles sized according to the height of the dog. There are both broad and high jumps, an A-frame to climb over, an elevated dog walk to

traverse, a teetering seesaw to walk or run across, a table to pause on, and an open tunnel to go through. There is a closed tunnel, made of fabric that Sam must push his way through, a set of poles to weave, and double bar jumps to leap over. There is also a suspended window frame and a tire he must jump through, and an identified area of the ground where he must pause.

In trials, the obstacles are laid out in a course, and the handler runs along beside, behind, or in front of the performing dog. Handlers may not touch the dog at any time. The scoring is based on course length and the time taken to complete it. A time penalty is charged for minor infractions, and refusal to try an obstacle counts five points against the participating dog. Refusals are not permitted for dogs competing in the AX class.

Training of sorts can begin when Sam is an energetic pup. However, you shouldn't progress too rapidly or he will tire of the rote exercises and lose interest in the endeavor.

Build an A-frame using plywood, hinged in the center. Instead of setting it up with the peak several feet above ground level, lay it nearly flat on the ground with the center elevated a few inches over a brick lying sideways. Coax Sam to walk back and forth across it. Initially he will try to jump off the A-frame, but with positive enticement he will walk, then run across it on command. Reward him only when he crosses the obstacle from end to end, never when he jumps off the side. When he has mastered this obstacle, raise the center to the height of a cinder block.

The same idea can be used on the dog walk. Cut the plank to the full specified size, but leave it on the ground and encourage Sam to walk the entire length, getting on and off the plank only on the colored ends. When he has conquered this feat, raise the plank the width of a brick, then to the height of a cinder block. Don't concern yourself with speed when teaching Sam how to approach and conquer each obstacle. Speed comes with practice and repetition.

A seesaw can also be set up with a low central fulcrum, gradually raising it as Sam gets older and more confident. Enticement with treats and verbal encouragement should be given as he makes his way along a seesaw or dog walk, with praise and reward being reserved for his correct performance of the task.

Prevent Sam from making errors. Don't allow him to jump off the side of any equipment, even if it means physically directing him. Keep his focus on staying on the dog walk, crossover, and A-frame. Use your hand or, if necessary, his leash, as well as a morsel of food. Sometimes it's necessary to erect sideboards on seesaws, dog walks, and other obstacles to keep Sam properly on them. This is easily accomplished when he is small and the obstacle is close to the ground.

Tunnels may be a problem until Sam becomes accustomed to walking on plastic surfaces. Put a flat

Agility A-Frame being investigated by a couple of doubtful Beagles.

piece of plastic on the grass in the backyard, one with the feel of an agility tunnel. Encourage him to walk on it by offering a tidbit in the center. Once he realizes this surface isn't to be feared, the open tunnel or pipe tunnel should be easy.

If he's reluctant to enter a curved tunnel, set the open tunnel on a straight course and have a friend hold him at one end. Go to the opposite end and call to him. If necessary, crawl into the tunnel a short distance and coax him with a treat or drag the treat in front of him. A few such rewarded accomplishments should relieve his fear of entering an open tunnel, regardless of its configuration.

Closed or collapsed tunnels present a problem for most very young dogs, but these obstacles can be left until later, when Sam has more confidence. If you wish to teach Sam to go through a closed tunnel, simply add a few feet of floppy cloth material to a short pipe tunnel or ring. Crawl through the tunnel ahead of him the first time or two. He should have no trouble negotiating the open ring with the backside of it draped with cloth. Once he realizes that all he has to do is push his nose through first, and more importantly, that there is a treat on the other side, he'll take this obstacle in stride.

Hurdles and jumps of all types should be reserved for a later date when Sam is older. However, the *jump* command can be taught to very young puppies when they approach a two-by-four lying on edge on the ground.

Minimal-height jumps can be set up for practice. It's best to erect sideboards on the jump so Sam must jump or stop. To encourage him to take a jump, give the command as you toss his favorite treat over the low jump. If this doesn't work, put him on a 6-foot (2-m) leash and trot along beside him as you lead him to the jump. Give him the *jump* command and encourage him up and over with gentle upward pressure on the leash as you jump the barrier. When he successfully completes the jump, reward him with a yummy treat.

Distractions

Agility trials are spectator sports. They draw large audiences of interested onlookers. Probably the greatest problems to overcome are the distractions of fans, the smells and sounds of a strange environment, barking dogs, and crowds of whistling, shouting people cheering their favorites on to victory.

Concentration or focus on you and on the task at hand is an elusive but necessary quality of a successful agility dog. If Sam has a notable power of concentration and is not easily distracted, he should do very well indeed. Don't overwork him. Never let training exceed his interest span, and make agility training enjoyable for both you and your dog.

Repeat the exercise several times with a reward when he gets it right and not so much as a word when he makes an error. If repeated mistakes are made, discontinue schooling on that exercise and go to one he's already mastered. Always end his learning session on a positive note, with an exercise he's sure of, even if it's walking on a leash once around the yard. It's important for Sam to remember that each session ends with a special reward.

Enroll in a class if you haven't done so already. You can construct the various obstacles, dog walks, pause tables, and A-frames, and you can school Sam in correct performance of all individual exercises without the benefit of an agility club's input. However, to compete, Sam must learn to perform before a noisy crowd of people, other dogs, and all sorts of strange sounds and odors. This all takes practice and the aid of an agility club.

Tracking

AKC Tracking contests are great sport for the crafty Beagle nose. This event is not a continuation of the tracking required in advanced obedience trials. If Sam shows a talent for tracking and searching for various family members, you might wish to try him in formal tracking events. Special training, harness, equipment, and rules are used in these events.

Levels and Awards

Tracking Test/TD is for dogs more than six months old having not yet earned a Tracking Dog (TD), Tracking Dog Excellent (TDX), or Variable Surface Tracking (VST) title. The TD title is earned when a dog is certified by two judges as having passed a Tracking Test/TD.

The TD requirements include the following criteria. The track followed must be at least 440 yards to 500 yards (402–457 m) long, with each leg of the track at least 50 yards (46 m) long. The track must be 30 minutes to two hours old. A total of three to five turns are used, including both left and right turns. Specific rules govern where turns may be made, the degree of the turns, and any fences and boundaries that may be included in tracks. Parallel tracks can't be used and the proximity of other tracks is also governed by TD rules, as are the obstacles that are allowable in TD tests.

A Tracking Test/TDX is available to dogs that have already earned a TD title. The TDX title is awarded to dogs having been certified by two judges to have passed a TDX test.

In TDX competition, the length of track is increased to 800 to 1,000 yards (732–914 m), but the length of each leg remains at 50 yards (46 m). The track age is increased to three

Tracking is a natural extension of trailing.

hours to five hours old and five to seven turns at various angles are used. Crosstracks, obstacles, and specific articles are included in this test to increase its complexity.

VST verifies the dog's ability to recognize and follow human scent while adapting to changing scenting conditions. Each track has a minimum of three different surfaces, including vegetation and two areas devoid of vegetation, such as concrete, asphalt, gravel, sand, hardpan, or mulch. No obstacles are used in this test, but tracks may be laid out through distractions, such as buildings, breezeways, shelters, and open garages.

There are four articles used in the VST test, each of which is made of a material different from the others, and all of which may be easily picked up by the dog. They are leather, plastic, metal, and fabric.

Beagle Careers

Beagles are hunting dogs, right? Their career opportunities are associated with scenting and finding rabbits or the hole into which the bunny disappeared, right? Well, not quite. It's been my pleasure to observe Beagles in action in a few other career positions as well.

Drug Detection Dogs

In this highly specialized career, the Beagle is trained to detect certain organic odors. Drugs, such as marijuana, cocaine, and others that are sometimes smuggled into the United States, are not easily detected when included in personal luggage or hidden in vehicles, campers, and boats. Sometimes, federal drug enforcement agencies use Beagles' acute olfactory senses to identify these drugs by teaching the dogs to react in a special way when the odors are detected.

Recently, when going through customs in Brussels, Belgium, I was surprised to meet a Beagle standing beside a customs guard. As we walked past, the robust oversized male did a cursory smell of my pockets, our bags, and my wife's purse. Appreciating the dog's thoroughness, I spoke to him. My brief comments seemed to stimulate his interest, causing him to go over my pockets and bag a second time. Satisfied, he then walked back to his handler, sat down, and waited for his next customer. I remarked that I felt much better with a dog sniffing my bag from the outside than a customs' agent rifling through the inside.

Fruit and Vegetable Detection

Beagles have terrific noses and are trained to identify virtually any type of odor. We were in Honolulu, waiting for an inter-island flight, as we watched a Beagle working. Each bag that came into the customs area was sniffed and apparently approved. All at once, the diminutive little hound furiously began to whine and scratch at one bag. The agricultural official sent the bag and owner

Beagles have wonderful scent distinction.

to another room, where presumably the owner was asked to explain why the suitcase full of raw fruit was being brought into the state in violation of Hawaiian quarantine laws.

In these types of detection, the dog is trained to detect certain specific organic scents. The method used to train these incredible dogs to detect particular odors is simply a continuation of the scent training described previously. Instead of searching for an object or a human odor, they are trained to search for objects having a fruity odor or the unmistakable odor of certain illegal drugs.

Therapy Dogs

A Beagle's temperament is well suited for a therapeutic visitation dog, one of the most enjoyable jobs you and Sam can find. Therapy dogs aren't just friendly dogs off the streets that happen in to a nursing home, hospice, or care center. They are beautifully socialized, well-mannered, clean, loving dogs that lick many hands and a few faces, sit on an occasional lap, and sometimes play with the residents. They make the day a little brighter for shut-ins, lift spirits, and motivate residents to interact.

I've seen these little dogs charm Alzheimer's disease victims in day care homes on several occasions. The soft and friendly Beagle is custom-made to bridge the gap between reality and the incognizant minds of these unfortunate people.

Beagles seem to love to share their personalities with incapacitated people and dote on the tenderness offered by those persons. Many care-home residents previously had dogs at home, loved them, and miss them terribly. In a friendly Beagle's soft brown eyes, they recall their favorite dog and reminisce about the good times of the past. In an affectionate Beagle's tongue, these unfortunate people relive the devoted response they received when speaking to and petting their dogs.

This story from Kris Kraeuter of Brushy Run Beagles tells of a situation that illustrates the Beagle personality.

"At a recent dog show, one of our Beagle girls was waiting patiently at ringside for her turn to show. Lilly is not yet a registered therapy dog. The show was a large, crowded, noisy indoor event, but the hounds were tolerant of children, all of whom petted and fussed over the cute little Beagles. Quietly, a woman approached us pushing a wheelchair, and in it was a severely retarded adult gentleman. Lilly had never seen a wheelchair before, nor had she been exposed to a handicapped or mentally challenged person. The man leaned over and began stroking her soft ears, whispering affectionately, and Lilly loved his attention.

"The caregiver said with tears in her eyes that she had never seen this man respond so quickly and completely to any other creature, man or animal.

"The following day, Whimsie, one of our youngest hounds, pulled a similar trick. Without invitation, she climbed onto the lap of a legally blind, wheelchair-bound former show judge. Each of them thoroughly enjoyed those moments of puppy kisses and stroking."

Seniors, physically handicapped, and mentally challenged residents, both children and adults, appreciate canine visits. There are three beneficiaries to each such encounter: every person your Beagle visits receives pleasure from the encounter; Sam is gratified by the attention he receives; and most of all, you have the joy and satisfaction of contributing.

Dog visitation brings something of the outside world to the otherwise boring lives of thousands every day. To gauge the benefits of a dog visiting a hospice and spending a small part of a day visiting the terminally ill, just ask those patients which visitors they enjoy the most.

The best-known therapy dog organization is The Delta Society, an international resource for the human-animal bond. This organization is dedicated to expanding the awareness of the positive effect animals can have on human health and development. It was established in 1977 in Portland, Oregon and has grown annually since that time. Its name came from the fourth letter of the Greek alphabet, D (δ). The triangle represents the relationship among pet owners, pets, and caregivers. Early Delta Society members were from the veterinary and human health professions and universities. Their objective was and still is to research the beneficial effect of pets on the general population, and more particularly, how these pets positively affect human health and well-being.

The Delta Society is also involved with the Hearing Dog Resource Center and Assistance Dogs and established the first screening criteria for pets in these programs. It publishes a number of newsletters and a home study course for volunteers who are interested in visitation programs. Their *People and Pets* activity is probably the most used American resource for therapy dogs and their handlers.

Some therapy dog organizations, such as Therapy Dogs of Vermont, take their dogs to various institutions; some are in costumes, some do tricks, and others just sit to be petted. They also visit meetings of scouts, schools, and universities when asked.

Besides being even-tempered and outgoing, therapy dogs should be more than one year old, healthy, well-groomed, and up-to-date on immunizations. It really helps if Sam responds to the fundamental obedience commands as well, and naturally, he should not be aggressive. Sam should be certified by an agency, such as The Delta Society or Therapy Dogs International, which also provides liability insurance and temperament testing. Some agencies then evaluate the dog and handler as they work with another certified team. (See Useful Addresses and Literature, page 193.)

Chapter Eleven

The Hunting Beagle

Good Scents

Beagles are rabbit dogs, right? Well, mostly perhaps, but they're just sensible scenting hounds. Kris Kraeuter of Brushy Run Beagles relates how her Beagles respond to pheasant scent. Her hounds will trail a running pheasant in the same manner they follow a rabbit track scent, but when vocalizing, there will be a slightly different tone to their voices. They will push the birds through heavy cover and eventually will flush them into the open at the edge of a field, where the birds usually will take wing. Most of these efficient little dogs will retrieve the birds as well.

Last year while pheasant hunting, Sassy trailed and flushed several ringnecks for Jack Kraeuter and followed one flying bird back into the brush, where she caught the pheasant and dutifully retrieved it, unharmed, to a very pleased owner. All present were amused at the sight of the 13.5-inch Beagle hauling that big ringneck rooster uphill and across the fields. Sassy is one member of a private pack that consists of quality conformation Beagles that also have proven to be very respectable hunters. Other members of the pack include an AKC conformation champion and several Beagles with AKC championship points and major show wins.

Beagles have great noses. They use their scenting ability superbly and few breeds can surpass them when it comes to scenting game.

Scent, smell, and *odor* are words similarly defined; there's no clear distinction between them and, under some circumstances, the three words are synonymous. Sometimes *scent* is a noun, in which case it means an animal's esoteric odor, a property that's difficult for humans to perceive, but quite real for the perceptively nosy Beagle. *Scenting* is a verb used to describe a dog's ability to follow animal scents or to identify the scents of particular substances.

Odor is a noun used to describe a property more easily recognized by humans, and s*mell* is a verb used synonymously with *sniff*, or sometimes it's a noun synonymous with *odor.*

While all animals possess a sense of smell, some species are gifted with greater scent determination or scenting ability than others, and *Canis familiaris* is among those species with the finest-tuned olfactory apparatus. Within that species, certain breeds of dogs have more acute scenting proclivity than others. This is true partly because scenting ability has been a major criterion for selective breeding. Individuals within a breed have scenting talents superior to others of that breed as well.

A large percentage of the canine brain is involved with scents; dogs have excellent olfactory sense. Scientists have estimated that dogs have 40 times more olfactory cells than are found in humans.

At a very early age, Sam's good scent discrimination is already at work. Whelped with his eyes sealed shut, this Beagle pup used his scenting ability to find his mother's mammary glands and even to locate a favorite nipple. A tiny puppy's olfactory system enables him to recognize the scent of a particular human, differentiate between people, and recognize strangers.

Field trial Beagle hesitates to pose for the camera.

Animal Scent

Have you ever wondered what gives various substances different smells? The oils of various fruits and vegetables are quite aromatic and easily detected by rudimentary human sniffers. Likewise, oils in various animal tissues give each beast its own unique smell, some of which are quite easily detected, and others that are more subtle. Organic vegetable or animal material has more distinguishable scent than inorganic or mineral substances. Most of us can differentiate between the smell of a sheep and that of an orange. However, once the animal or vegetable is gone from the immediate area, how is Sam able to follow these scents, hours or even days later?

Humans have strong scents that are similar to one another, but are actually unique for each individual. The scent of a human is made up of oils from sebaceous glands of the skin, scales or flakes of skin debris, sweat, breath, and perhaps pheromones. Human scents vary by race, type of clothes worn, diet, personal hygiene, toiletries used, and other components. Your own peculiar scent is the means by which your Beagle recognizes you, even in the dark.

Scent Cone

This is an interesting concept, one that is easily understood and one that will give you a greater appreciation of how your Beagle follows a certain scent.

Imagine a hypothetical, continual source of odorous smoke, such as a smelly cigar. The smoking cigar is located in a vacuum jar where sufficient oxygen is available for combustion, but absolutely no movement of air exists. In such a case, the smoke never leaves its source, and the air immediately adjacent to the cigar becomes saturated with smoke.

In a natural setting, even in the absence of wind, air is dynamic, always on the move; air currents are always discernible.

Now imagine the same lighted cigar in this natural setting. The smoking cigar is positioned on the ground in an open field. Imperceptible air currents are moving everywhere, but a general directional current prevails. This current carries the smoke away from the cigar in a three-dimensional pattern, which takes the shape of a cone. Cigar smoke is quite concentrated at its source, which is the tip of the cone. The smoke becomes less

dense or more dilute as it is carried by the prevailing air currents away from the source and higher into the atmosphere.

Let's put a jackrabbit in place of the smelly cigar. Mr. Rabbit's body odor, when subjected to natural air currents, produces a similar scent cone.

A dog's instinctive scenting ability involves more than the ability to detect the presence of the rabbit's airborne scent. Sam also can measure the density or concentration of the scent and can instantly distinguish the rabbit's scent from the hundreds of other scents in the area. Once the jackrabbit's airborne scent is perceived, Sam moves into the scent cone and follows the rabbit scent from low concentration toward high concentration. Just how he does this is only conjecture. When he has followed the scent cone to its source, he's found Jack the rabbit.

Airborne Scent

Airborne scent is the body odor falling from or swept from an animal's body and carried by air currents. All animals produce body odors that become airborne and are characteristic of that particular species. This scent is a personal vapor that envelops and follows the animal all its life.

Ambient warmth enhances odors by increasing the volatility of the scent, breaking it into small airborne particles. These particles remain suspended in the air for a period of time after the animal has passed. Airborne scent is most concentrated near its source and becomes diluted with distance and with increased air movement.

With his highly sensitive olfactory cells, the dog can trace the airborne scent of an animal and follow it for lengthy periods of time.

Generally, airborne scent is detected when the source of the scent is upwind of the dog. When the rabbit has passed through an area, its scent will be carried by air currents to ditches, water, rocks, trees, and other vegetation. It tends to be trapped by or cling to these objects for a time, then is carried away gradually by the wind. Therein lies a tracking problem. How does a Beagle efficiently find a rabbit when its scent hangs on the landscape for a while, then is gradually released?

Airborne scent is fickle! If the rabbit is moving, the tip of its scent cone shifts with its every movement. Sam's ability to work out the highest concentration of scent works well as long as the bunny moves in a straight line. Have you ever seen a rabbit hop in a straight line? Being prey, it instinctively runs helter-skelter and in circles even when not pursued by a Beagle. Sam's job would be quite difficult except for his other scenting abilities. This is why a good tracking Beagle keeps his nose to the ground, so he can follow the ground and track scents and not the deceptive airborne scent.

Beagle pack busily seeking new scents.

Ground Scent

The scent of broken, bruised, and crushed leaves and grasses, together with the scent of disturbed or packed soil, are the major components of the ground scent that is left behind as an animal moves through an area. Cold ground tends to hold scent in place, while warmer ground causes the scent to rise and diffuse. A track lightly covered with snow is easier for a Beagle to follow than one laid on warm ground.

Ground scent concentration begins to fade soon after the animal has walked by. It diffuses in every direction due to the dynamic tendency of air to move, dilute, and equalize the concentration of such vapors. When the rabbit hops by, its airborne scent is the first to leave, then its ground trail, and finally, its track scent, which is further defined below.

Track Scent

Each species has its own scent. Hares, cottontail rabbits, squirrels, large game, and the various birds have scents peculiar to their species. As they move over the ground, they leave their scents, which are further enhanced by their periodic dropping of excretions, bits of fur, feathers, and in the case of a wounded animal, blood.

Track scent is a particular odor composed of a combination of microscopic scales falling from the animal's skin. It contains minute pieces of fur and oils from its scent glands, footpads, and skin glands.

These scents are mixed with the odors emanating from its excretions clinging to its fur and, probably, pheromones. As the rabbit moves along, its toenails dig into and disturb the soil, and some of its personal scent is pressed into the ground and cover. Grasses, leaves, and weeds are crushed or broken and the rabbit's personal scent is mixed with the scent of injured plants, leaving further evidence of the quarry's trail. Without realizing it, a complex track, smelling like no other, has been left behind, following the rabbit wherever it goes. This mixture of smells becomes the rabbit's track scent, the authentic signature of the animal.

Track scent is more apparent when the ground temperature is cool but warming. You know the aromas of the kitchen increase when meat or vegetables are cooked. Heat tends to bring out the scent from these organic materials, causing it to disseminate into the entire house. The same thing happens to track scent. Cooler temperatures hold the scent on the ground for longer periods of time and hotter weather causes the scent to diffuse into the air.

Have you ever noticed how a bar of soap has little odor when dry, then when you take it into the shower, the room instantly is filled with the soap's fragrance? The same phenomenon is seen when dew is evaporating during the early morning hours. The dew saturates the scent trail immediately above the track. By the same token, a light rain following the laying of a track will freshen the scent and make it easier for Sam to follow. Track scent may remain in place for hours or even several days when the weather is foggy, misty, and windless. Under those conditions, scent will rise slowly from the track and remain a fraction of an inch above the ground. Hot weather, especially a hot, dry wind, will drive track scent into the atmosphere within minutes.

Scenting Is Natural

When you're walking in the country, if you're like most of us, you instantly detect the smell of wildflowers, sage, pine, and other strong natural odors. Similarly, Sam will recognize many scents that escape you. He identifies the scents of crushed ground cover, disturbed soil, and various animals as easily as you recognize a wild onion when you step on it.

You can see his scent-memory function. He may be leading you on the day-old track of a rabbit, a track that is invisible to you, then interrupt this tracking to investigate the fresher track of a ground bird, then, after a few seconds, turn back and pick up the more interesting bunny trail and continue tracking.

While he's seeking or following an animal trail, observe his head attitude, ear set, tail carriage, and other distinctive body signals. A Beagle on a hot trail will begin to *feather*, which

Measuring a pack Beagle.

is an excited twitching of his tail. This body language soon should mean something to you; his every little inconspicuous sign tells you what he's thinking.

If safe to do so, let him investigate off lead, but remember the Beagle's propensity to split when a fresh, interesting track is discovered. Experts have stated more than once that Beagles' motivation to hunt often overwhelms the desire to please their masters. Unless you have great faith in Sam's training, don't allow him to track on his own in strange country. He isn't apt to honor *No Trespassing* signs, and once he's gained cover, he's not apt to look back to see if you're following.

Gundog

If you plan to hunt with Sam, begin some preliminary gun training early. Acquire a toy cap pistol, and when he's standing across the yard from you, hold the gun behind you, point it away from him toward the ground, and fire. If he's startled, that's normal, and should be ignored. If you show no excitement or fear, he isn't apt to be alarmed. Never fire any gun close to his head; not only will the concussion frighten him, the noise may cause hearing impairment.

Gun safety rules are beyond the scope of this book, but this subject should be thoroughly reviewed before any gun training is begun.

After he's comfortable with the noise of the cap gun, try your small-gauge shotgun. With Sam on a long lead and some distance away, fire the shotgun in the opposite direction from him. Generally, Beagles aren't gun-shy, but before you take your dog and gun to the field, you should know exactly what to expect from your Beagle when you fire.

AKC Beagle Field Trials

These events are held by member clubs under AKC rules. Judging is performed by AKC-licensed judges, who strive for uniformity in everything from ribbon color and entry forms to judges' decisions. The actual trial is managed by the member club's Field Trial Committee, which is appointed from its members.

Classes and Awards

The AKC trial is run under one of four procedures (other organizations' trials follow different formats):
• Braces on Wild Rabbit or Hare.
• Small Packs on Wild Rabbit or Hare.
• Small Packs Option on Wild Rabbit or Hare.
• Large Packs on Hare.

Beagle field trial officials and competitors are quite concerned with Beagle size, and rules for measuring, tables, measuring apparatus, and certification of the Beagle's size receive a lot of ink in the AKC rules.

The Beagles are run according to their sex and size (under 13 inches and over 13 inches but not exceeding 15 inches). If insufficient dogs are entered, sexes are run together. No Beagle can be entered in more than one class. If six or more Beagles are entered in a class, the winning Beagles are awarded field championship points according to this schedule:
• 1 point to the first-place winner for each starter.
• ½ point to the second-place Beagle for each starter.

- ⅓ point to the third-place Beagle for each starter.
- ¼ point to the fourth-place Beagle for each starter.

A starter is an eligible hound that meets all rule specifications.

Championship

To earn an AKC Field Champion title, a Beagle must have won three first places and accumulated a total of 120 points in classes of not less than six starters.

If this same Beagle earns a conformation title of Show Champion, it will be designated as a Dual Champion (DC).

If the same Beagle wins an Obedience Trial Champion (OTCh) title, it will be designated a Triple Champion (TC).

National Brace Championship Field Trials, National Small Pack Option Championship Field Trials, and National Large Pack Championship Field Trials are held annually for the big winners.

Another competition recently added to the beagling lineup is the NBC Triple Challenge, discussed on page 130.

Field Trial Objectives

Beagle field trials are designed to allow these talented hunting dogs an opportunity to perform the duties for which they were originally bred. They earn their competitive placements by being eager, determined, and willing to work out problems encountered through deliberate and efficient action.

To win, a Beagle must have a keen nose, a sound body, intelligence, and enthusiasm. Winners display quality in breeding as well as ability. They must be free of faulty actions, as specified by the trial rules and regulations.

Judges in Beagle field trials are given the responsibility of placing dogs that, if bred, will improve the breed. They should make their selections based on the future of Beagles' usefulness in both field trials and hunting. To do this, they consider the Beagle's searching ability, independence, and ranging. The Beagle is also judged on his progress on the trail or accuracy and accomplishment of pursuit rather than simply following a trail. Efficiency of regaining the trail when he is lost or checked is also judged.

When positively on the scent trail, the Beagle gives tongue, and this too is judged. A Beagle should listen and honor a pack mate that is giving voice. In trail language, this is termed *harking in*. Then, when the quarry's trail is identified, each Beagle should follow it and not the scent of his pack mates. Sam's independent ability to trust his own good nose and not follow the sounds of other Beagles' tongues is important.

A Beagle's endurance is a judged feature, as is his adaptability to the various scenting conditions. His compatibility with other dogs running in the same class is evaluated, as is his patience and yeomanlike manner of pursuit of the quarry. Patience and

Pack of Beagles hot on the trail.

determination are among the highest qualities of a good field trial Beagle.

Intelligence and experience are esoteric qualities that allow a good Beagle to compete with minimum wasted effort and to run as efficiently as possible.

Faults

• Quitting is a relative term that may be caused by problems ranging from fatigue to refusal to run. A lack of desire to hunt also may cause a Beagle to quit. This is perhaps the most serious fault a field Beagle can display.

• Backtracking is the error a Beagle makes when he follows a trail the wrong way for more than a few seconds. If the mistake is temporary, and quick correction is made, most judges will show leniency.

• Ghost trailing is running on an imaginary track. Some Beagles are fairly adept at this deception.

• Pottering or dawdling, with listless lack of true Beagle intent, is another fault.

• Babbling is the term used to describe the excessive tonguing some Beagles are guilty of when covering a trail over and over.

• Swinging is casting or ranging too far from the trail when a scent is lost or vague and is often the fault of a highly competitive Beagle.

• Skirting is the attempt of a Beagle to gain a lead on his competitors through avoiding tough cover by skirting around it and attempting to pick up the trail on the other side.

• Leaving checks is similar to swinging in that the Beagle fails to stay in the vicinity of the lost trail and bounds off with the hope of finding a new trail.

• Running mute is the lack of giving tongue when progressing on a track.

• Tightness of mouth is similar except that this fault is seen when the

Beagle quiets when pressed by competitors.

• Racing is the attempt to outrun competitors without regard for the trail. It is evidenced by overrunning turns in the trail, swinging, and so forth.

• Running hit or miss is similar to racing in that it describes the propensity to progress without keeping contact with the track.

• Lack of independence is common. If a Beagle watches competitors and allows them to lead, he is probably guilty of this fault.

• Bounding off is rushing away when a scent is picked up without determining the direction of the quarry.

Anatomy of a Field Trial

All these field trials are run by specific, rather strict organizational plans. Brace or pack mates are selected by a drawing of all dogs in the class. This drawing is a means to impartially set the running order of braces, trios, or packs. There are rules that address splitting classes in cases where large numbers are entered. Some fundamental organizational rules have been paraphrased here; complete rules are available from the organization sponsoring the event.

• A brace is a pair of hounds running together.

• A trio is three hounds running together.

• A pack is more than three hounds running together.

• The trial secretary calls the hounds and they have a set order in which to compete.

• The called Beagles are all kept on leashes until they are directed to begin.

• *Casting* is the term used to describe the beginning of a trial class. When the dogs are released to begin the search for game trails, they are said to be cast.

• They may be cast from a point decided by the judge unless they are kept on leash and taken to a place where game has been sighted. At this point they are said to be laid on line.

• Small packs consist of four to nine hounds run together, regardless of ownership, and they also are drawn by the secretary.

• Beagle packs are run as long as the judges deem necessary to select the hounds to compete in the next series. When sufficient series have run and the necessary eliminations have been made, the pack consisting of five to seven hounds in a Small Pack trial (five to nine hounds in a Small Pack Option trial) runs together as the Winners Pack.

• The Winners Pack is run, and dogs are eliminated by faults until two Beagles are selected to run as a brace, from which the judges select the top hound.

Small Pack Option

The principal difference between the Small Pack and Small Pack Option is that, in the Option, all Beagles must be tested for gun-shyness. This testing is done with blank cartridges and by a particular technique specifying that guns are fired only when the pack is on fresh scent and in pursuit of game.

Other minor differences specify that in the Small Pack Option, hounds aren't faulted for trailing small game other than the hare. In these trials, the Beagle's propensity to energetically drive his quarry and attempt to overtake it is considered a laudable objective. Ability and desire to hunt are of primary consideration, and judges are encouraged to give credit to hounds that are the best searchers and trail their quarry accurately when its track is found. More emphasis is also given to smooth running of the pack in judging the Small Pack Option hounds.

Other Trials

The AKC trials discussed above aren't the only tests of ability available to Beagles. There are AKC Beagle Derbies open to young dogs, and Sanctioned Beagle Field Trials may be offered by AKC member clubs. These trials are run by the same rules as other field trials, except that no championship points are awarded.

NBC Triple Challenge

First held in 1996, this event is sponsored by the National Beagle Club of America each May at Institute Farm, Aldie, Virginia.

The three-phase weekend event was initiated to recognize and promote the complete and versatile Beagle.

During the first phase, the hunting talents of each individual hound are evaluated in a brace format trial.

The Beagle's ability to contribute to the work of a pack afield is evaluated as well. During a three-hour stakes class, 30 Beagles are cast in

Trio of Beagles waiting for their turn.

one large pack to hunt rabbit followed by judges on horseback and handlers who follow on foot.

In the third phase, Beagles in the triple challenge are judged for conformation to the AKC breed standard.

Triple Challenge placements are awarded based on a combined point score earned through competition in all three phases of the event. A hound must be entered and compete in each phase of the event to be considered for points.

This event serves another purpose. It brings beaglers together! Representatives of the various factions within the breed join together with a common purpose, in the same place, to talk about a love they share, Beagles! Each attendee has the opportunity to offer compliments and complaints, and communication lines are wide open.

NBC Pack Trials

These traditional British beagling pack hunting events are held twice annually with performance stake classes in conjunction with conformation shows.

UKC Field Trials

The United Kennel Club (UKC) is very much involved with beagling. This registry has information available on their Large Pack and Small Pack Trials. (See Useful Addresses and Literature, page 193).

The rules are similar to those of the AKC, with minor differences. The points to attain a Field Champion are awarded differently from the AKC policy, and the UKC awards a Grand Field Champion title as well.

UKC positive beagle features: The UKC *Large Pack/Small Pack Beagle Handbook* lists some positive characteristics that are paraphrased here and are used in evaluating hounds in UKC competition.

Credit is given to hounds that consistently search for game in an eager, efficient, and intelligent manner.

While pursuing game, a hound must keep in close contact with the scent line. Recklessness, competitiveness, and eagerness to overtake game must never excuse a hound for continually losing the scent line.

A hunting hound must have a good nose to be able to operate under adverse conditions throughout the season, but a good nose shouldn't be confused with simply tonguing when the other hounds are quiet. Hounds must have the desire and ability brought about by correct conformation and conditioning, to hunt without showing undue signs of weariness or fatigue.

When working checks, a hound must show patience, intelligence, and the desire to account for his game. When a scent line is lost, a hound is expected to immediately return to the point of loss and diligently work to reclaim the line.

In the proper balance, speed is an asset for keeping pressure on the game. Hounds must also be honest with their mouth, tongue freely while advancing, and not open at all when scent is lacking. Desire is the quality that drives a hound to succeed when the going gets tough. It's a combination of strength, heart, and determination to pursue the quarry.

A true mark of a Beagle's intelligence is his ability to smoothly and quickly adapt to different situations. This ability will be shown by his adaptation to varying terrains, different pack mates, different covers, and weather condition changes.

Faults listed by the UKC are quite similar to the AKC faults discussed previously.

UKC Hunting Beagle Event

Closely resembling an actual hunting experience, this event is held in the field under hunting conditions. Four Beagles with their handlers are grouped to form a cast. The dogs are required to search for and start a rabbit. The Beagles then run the rabbit as fast as scenting conditions allow and when it is overtaken, the Beagles circle their quarry.

The Beagles are scored on a point system that considers their opening on the track and their position on the line as they run.

The UKC hunting Beagle program has grown since 1990 to include nearly 100 approved clubs in 20 states and Canada. Many excellent hunting Beagles have been awarded Champion titles and will be recognized as rabbit hounds of the highest caliber.

CKC Trials

The Canadian Kennel Club is an all-breed registry that holds bench shows, field trials, and other canine events.

ARHA Trials

The American Rabbit Hound Association is less than 15 years old and functions in the registry of Beagles, Basset Hounds, and Harriers. This registry holds different types of field trials as well as conformation bench shows.

PKC Trials

The Professional Kennel Club is quite active in Coonhound events, and in 1999 it also began registering Beagles with an eye toward holding Beagle field trials in the near future. As the title of the organization indicates, cash prizes are awarded for placement in their trials.

NABR Trials

North American Beagle Registry began a few years ago and presently holds several different types of field trials.

Chapter Twelve

The Conformation Beagle

Pedigrees and Registration

Have you heard an uninformed person make a statement like this? "My dog is a papered thoroughbred; she's got a pedigree as long as your arm. I think her stud was a grand champion or something. I could show her if I wanted to, but I decided to save her for breeding." An example of gross confusion of terms compounded by incognizance!

Thoroughbred literally means thoroughly trained or skilled, or animals bred from the best blood of a long line. By that definition, the word could refer to purebred dogs, but rarely is the term so used except by the *naive*. Usually, *thoroughbred* refers to the specific breed of racehorses having their origin in Great Britain. Thoroughbred also is occasionally used to describe a person of enviable culture and quality. *Purebred* is the word of choice to describe Rosy's Beagle ancestry.

Indeed, any dog could have a *pedigree*, because that word refers to a list of ancestors. Every nondescript mutt has ancestors; the prob-lem is that nobody maintains their names on a list. Theoretically, it's possible for someone to have recorded the names of each of a mutt's progenitors to make a genealogical tree, which would be her pedigree.

The length of Rosy's genealogical chart has no bearing on her quality. A three- or four-generation pedigree, or the ancestors listed thereon, offers no proof of genetic superiority. When a pedigree is stippled on both sire and dam's sides with names and titles of outstanding show dogs, one would expect the Beagle in question to have a better than average chance of finishing in the purple, but there is no assurance. Rosy is an individual; if she has inherited the best features of her sire and dam, and if she is interested, properly trained, and well handled, she may be a winner.

Shows and Their Purpose

The term *benched show* refers to shows in which the dogs (except puppies) are displayed to the public

AKC Champion Beagle on a Jr. Showmanship bench.

on platforms set up in individual stalls or designated spots when they are not in the show ring being judged. In unbenched shows, the dogs are not kept in specific places, and may be found anywhere on the show grounds.

The world's first dog show was held in Great Britain in 1859. The first all-breeds show in the United States was held in Detroit, Michigan in 1875.

A dog show is the place where conformity to the breed standard is proven. Conformation or bench shows were begun by organizations to maintain studbooks of the various purebreds, to keep pedigrees, and to help breed clubs develop standards. In other words, dog shows are

designed to standardize the breed, to publish this standard, and to promote breeding dogs that meet the standard.

At the same time, field trials and other performance events are staged to assure that the dogs being exhibited in shows retain superior working attributes.

Over the years dog shows and performance events have each assumed an identity of their own. Beagler factions favoring either event have enjoyed differences of opinion, and neither is necessarily right or wrong. Similar factions are found in nearly every breed fancy, even when the lines between two fields of thought are not as well defined as they are among Beagle admirers.

Beagle performance events and conformation shows were and still are of equal importance. It's no sin to produce show Beagles exclusively any more than it's a mistake to run all your Beagles in field trials. Common ground is plentiful, and more beaglers are finding it.

AKC Functions

In the United States, two major all-breed registries exist, the AKC and UKC. The largest and most influential all-breed dog club in the United States is the American Kennel Club, commonly known as the AKC. It came into being in 1884 with the purpose of registering and maintaining studbooks for dogs of all breeds. Its other functions are to sanction dog events of various types and to promote responsible dog ownership. In its 116 years, it has become a fantastic canine resource, offering a full line of education and information and maintaining libraries and museums as well. However, the AKC is a registry service, not an organization of and for breeders. It doesn't set breeder standards and isn't responsible for uniform practices by dog breeders.

If a dog is *registered* with one of the all-breed organizations, it means the dog's parents and progenitors were purebred. Neither the AKC nor the UKC has regulatory functions except in the events it sanctions. Registration in either organization doesn't assure that the dog is of superior conformation, and does not imply inspection by that organization. Neither should the notation *registered* suggest good health or superior personality, attitude, or aptitude.

AKC dog show judges are trained and licensed by that registry but are selected and paid by the clubs sponsoring the event. Trophies and ribbons are standardized by the registries but are imprinted and bought by the clubs.

Conformation Shows

Dog shows, in a way, are akin to beauty contests. Their object is to judge each purebred Beagle against the breed standard, considering size, colors, coat, conditioning, bone structure, gait, and personality. The Beagle standard was written and adopted by the National Beagle Club (NBC), which is composed of a regular membership consisting of a local SPO (Small Pack Option) group and a nationwide collection of Beagle and Basset enthusiasts who are affiliated with the NBC registered foot hunts or organized packs. The NBC also has a supporting membership composed of conformation show beaglers from across the nation. The AKC subsequently adopted this standard, which describes the perfect or ideal Beagle.

The NBC is the umbrella organization for our breed, and its address is included in the Useful Addresses section on page 193. State or regional clubs are composed of Beagle breeders and fanciers with common interests centered around betterment of the breed.

Show Eligibility

All AKC-registered Beagles six months of age or older are allowed to compete in AKC conformation shows except those standing more than 15 inches tall. Other disqualifying features found in Beagles and all other AKC-registered breeds include spayed bitches, castrated males, retained testicles, lameness, and a few others.

Puppy Evaluation and Training

Rosy is six months old and you're anxious to get her into the ring. Before entering her in a conformation show, there are a few important facts you should know. Write to or call the AKC, or bring up the AKC web page on your computer. (See Useful Addresses and Literature, page 193.) Obtain the Beagle standard and judge for yourself whether or not Rosy conforms to this standard. Then have a beagling friend informally compare Rosy to the ideal Beagle in the standard just to be sure you haven't overlooked anything. If you belong to a local Beagle club, ask a member-breeder with showing experience to fault Rosy or point out to you the flaws recognized in Rosy's conformation or character.

If Rosy has good conformation, has a bubbly personality, is a bit of a ham, and dotes on attention, she may just have the makings of a good show dog. The next step is to write or call the AKC and ask for Rules Applying to Dog Shows, get an entry blank from your club's show steward, and continue with Rosy's show career.

Before you go much further, be sure Rosy is adequately trained. Oh yes, show training is part of the dog showing game! Rosy must be polite and obedient when she is led into the ring. She must focus on her handler carefully to see what is expected of her. She is expected to gait well, and she must stand properly and allow the judge to physically inspect her body.

Rosy should be taken to and from the ring at heel or on a close lead. You, as handler, must listen to the judge for specific instructions from that point on and never be guilty of watching the gallery, playing with Rosy, or waving to a friend in the crowd. Concentrate on the judge's voice and the business at hand. Split your focus between the judge and Rosy; pay no attention to other dogs in the ring or their handlers. When you are instructed to take Rosy up and back, she should be gaited at a rather quick pace and should keep the leash relatively taut but not appear to be pulling.

Rosy should *stack* easily when she is placed on the judge's table to display her many attributes, such as the Beagle's tight feet, short straight pasterns, and well-sprung ribs. She should be taught to stand quietly on a table for the judge's examination, and when the judge approaches, Rosy should allow her mouth to be opened without resistance. A friendly tail wag when the judge runs her hands over Rosy's ribs will always bring a smile of approval from the official.

A show dog and her handler should work together as a team, one dependent on the other; they should complement each other, not argue or nag their way around the ring. Training should take place between shows, not during the judging.

Many show-ring heartaches can be avoided by attending your all-breed club's show-training classes. These classes are designed to prepare both Rosy and you for conformation shows by instructing you in the art of dog handling and making suggestions for your Beagle's further training at home.

When a great Beagle enters the ring looking good and having all the right stuff on both ends of the lead, she should win, right? Not necessarily. Sometimes another dog catches the judge's eye and shows something that Rosy doesn't have, at least not yet.

Lee Cord of Londonderry-MC's Beagles tells of an interesting situation involving a Beagle named Paige who thought she had winning all figured out. Paige was performing flawlessly, but regularly took a back seat to a puppy that lacked experience. This pup wouldn't even allow the

A tough competitor in the show ring.

judge to examine her. The puppy acted up and obviously lacked training, but nevertheless always took the points.

One day when both dogs were in the ring, Paige uncharacteristically jumped high in the air, acting silly; she looked as if she never before had been in a show ring. Again, she took reserve, but it wasn't because she didn't try everything she'd seen the winning pup do. Friends asked Lee why Paige acted up; it was so unlike her, but Lee knew why. Perhaps Paige reasoned that the lack of training got the judge's attention, or maybe she felt that because she was going to get the second spot anyway, why shouldn't she have a little fun in the bargain!

Handlers

Handler is the title given to the person who shows the dog. In bred-by-exhibitor classes, only owners can handle their dogs. In most instances, the handler may be the owner or someone who takes the owner's place. A handler's experience and ability are extremely important factors in the outcome of any dog show.

Professionals

Eventually, you may decide to hire a professional handler to show Rosy. Usually, this decision is made after her puppy-class experience, because few professionals handle young, unproven dogs.

Professional dog handlers are part of showing, but they aren't necessary if you have patience and determination and if you accept criticism and instruction willingly. You seldom will attend a point show that has no professional handlers, and when they're present, they're a force to be reckoned with. Years of experience handling hundreds of dogs give them a decided advantage over owner-handlers. However, most judges' visibility isn't completely clouded by the relaxed, professional presence on the other end of the lead. If Rosy is an outstanding dog with the qualities being sought, you can win in spite of overwhelming odds.

Junior Handlers

Children who aspire to handle the family Beagle should begin by attending junior handling classes offered by your all-breed club. They can progress to handling Rosy in puppy matches, from there to junior handling classes, and then to handling her in point shows. From such an inauspicious beginning are born many licensed professional handlers.

No preference is given to children who handle their family dogs, but there is something about a neat, well-disciplined child leading a well-behaved Beagle that appeals to judge and audience alike.

Handler Preparation

Children or adult owners should first attend a number of dog shows, regardless of what breeds are being exhibited. Take a seat in the gallery and observe the various handlers carefully; watch their techniques, their positions, their attitudes, and their ring presence. See how each dog is displayed to its best advantage.

You'll see experienced handlers in conservative dress and action, staying in the background, always seeking to place their dogs in the judge's field of vision. The handler coaxes and draws out her Beagle's best points, without calling attention to herself. She wears no gaudy or jangling jewelry or accessories that might catch the judge's eye and divert attention from her dog.

Watch the handler move with her dog, smoothly accelerating and slowing, keeping enough space between her dog and herself to allow the judge a clear vision of the Beagle. The best trick of a great handler is to make this job look natural and easy, letting the judge see the best qualities of her Beagle without getting in the way. In order to accomplish that feat, she must be well aware of her Beagle's attributes. A good handler always has a smile for the judge, but her mannerisms are conservative, like her clothes. Her Beagle always looks the best she can, sometimes better than she really is. If an experienced handler has an outstanding dog, the team will look almost perfect.

Handler errors often are the cause for Rosy not getting the attention of the judge, rather than any conformational fault your Beagle may have.

Show Entries

The AKC is particular about show entries. Everything must be in order on the dog's registration, and the application and payment must be correctly filed and mailed by a deadline date.

Judging

A show judge's job is a tough one. She must compare every dog to the Beagle standard and pick only one Beagle as the best in the class. She must consider the age and sometimes overlook the scars of dogs in

Standing like a champion.

the class, but she can only judge what is actually before her. In other words, she shouldn't place a young Beagle above a mature competitor because the youngster probably will mature into a better specimen. Neither can she put an older dog up because she remembers judging that particular dog in the past when it looked better.

Unfortunately, Rosy doesn't show exactly the same in any two shows. Even though she's the same dog with the same attributes and faults and the same handler, her placement varies according to each judge's opinion.

Dog shows are designed to bring phenotypic uniformity (the Beagle's manifest characteristics) to a breed. Although performance isn't a part of conformation shows, judges must consider it when they select the best Beagles in a class. Theoretically, each competitor is judged according to his or her probable ability to participate in the various special activities for which Beagles were developed.

Conformation show judges don't watch the class of Beagles hunt, work under a gun, or perform in field trials. In other words, many important genotypic Beagle characteristics must be taken for granted by show judges. They can only choose the winning Beagle in the class by selecting the best physical representative of the breed.

A judge is rarely able to see beyond Rosy's temperament, appearance, coat, color, bone structure, angulation, and gait. Her size

and proportion can be easily ascertained, but it's difficult to tell if Rosy has the packing characteristics to allow her to hunt in packs or braces. Her strength and personality usually can be evaluated only to a degree, and her scenting ability and trainability in the various performance events also may elude even the most astute judge.

Dogs compete against the same sex in each class, but at a point, the judge must decide whether dog *A* is a better male than bitch *B* is a female. That's almost as tough as deciding the winner of a group. Is Beagle *C* a better specimen of the Beagle breed than Foxhound *D* is of the Foxhound breed?

Another difficult feature of judging is comparing the personalities of dogs present against the requirements listed in the standard. How do you judge such things as courage, willingness, or stamina? Judging is a tough job!

Types of Shows

Like Beagles, dog shows come in a variety of types with various purposes.

Fun Matches

Local all-breed clubs may hold a puppy match to culminate their show-schooling classes. Such a match is often the first exposure to the discipline required in actual shows. It gives the owner-handler an idea of how effective the preparation of the past weeks has been. A club member who has considerable experience usually judges the matches, but sometimes an AKC judge will help out as well.

Puppy matches are instructional and always offer suggestions or critiques to both dogs and handlers. This is the place for novices to gain knowledge and to compare their dogs with other novices' dogs. Ribbons may be awarded, but championship points are not earned for wins in a puppy match.

Junior Showmanship

If a child between the ages of 10 and 16 shows interest in showing and you wish to promote this interest, junior showmanship (often called junior handling) is the place to begin. However, it isn't the place for a child with absolutely no knowledge of dogs or dog shows. It's a place where the child can get hands-on experience with the show ring, judge, and showing rules.

Dogs shown in these contests must be AKC-registered and eligible to compete in dog shows or obedience trials. Classes within this contest include the Novice Class for those kids who have not won three first-place awards in that class, and the Open Class for those who have previously won three first places in the Novice Class.

These contests are competitions of young handlers against one another. The behavior of their dogs secondarily affects the final outcome of the contest because this behavior reflects the ability of a novice handler to control and exhibit her Beagle to her best advantage. A well-trained Champion Beagle may behave wonderfully, but the child-handler is judged according to her ability to bring to the judge's attention all that the dog has to offer. Generally, a better trained dog will make a junior handler look better. However, a beautiful and well-behaved dog may make a sloppy novice look poor in comparison to a novice handler who is doing a great job exhibiting a poor quality Beagle. A neatly attired, self-confident youngster with a well-trained, exuberant Beagle is bound to place high.

Sanctioned by the AKC, Junior Showmanship contests are intended to be instructional and are the way many kids start in the dog fancy. Clubs award ribbons and certificates to winners, and these proofs of ability are always cherished by those children.

Sanctioned Matches

All-breed dog clubs and some specialty clubs hold matches designed to accommodate novice handlers and their purebred dogs in an authentic show environment. Often, matches precede a club's point show.

Sanctioned matches are more formal than puppy matches and less formal than point shows. Only AKC-registered dogs compete, and point-show conditions prevail throughout the match, but no championship points are awarded.

Judging usually is done by qualified AKC judges because the event is sanctioned by that organization. The purpose of sanctioned matches is to give experience to and train both dogs and handlers for future point shows. AKC rules apply, but the contests are instructional, and the judges often spend time telling handlers how to improve their performance.

Point Shows

Governed by AKC rules, these formal shows are held under the direction of an AKC-licensed superintendent, with AKC licensed judges. They may be all-breed or specialty shows (one breed or group) and may be held in conjunction with other AKC events, such as obedience, field, or agility trials.

The AKC's *Rules Applying to Dog Shows*, a 60-page pamphlet, can be obtained from that organization. It leads you from the definition of a dog show through every step taken by a

Judge measuring length of ear.

member club to hold a show. This pamphlet is invaluable if you decide to follow this rewarding and fascinating hobby.

The scope of this Beagle handbook doesn't permit a discussion of all the rules pertaining to AKC Conformation shows and the methods of attaining the coveted Championship title. Instead, a brief discussion of show types, class structure, and point awards is included here.

Point shows are those that award championship points, which are accumulated by a dog to earn an AKC Champion of Record title. They may be all-breed shows or shows that are restricted to a single breed or a group, such as hounds or toys or American-bred dogs.

A single-breed show, held by a breed club, is the simplest type to describe. The classes available are as follows:
• Puppy Class is for nonchampion dogs between the ages of 6 months and 1 year and is often divided into 6- to 9-month and 9- to 12-month classes.
• Twelve-to-Eighteen-Month-Old (nonchampion) Class.
• Novice Class is made up of dogs six months or older that have not won three first prizes in the Novice Class nor accumulated any championship points.
• Bred-by-Exhibitor Class is designed for nonchampion dogs that are more than 6 months old and handled in the class by the breeder or spouse who is owner or co-owner of the dog.

- American-bred Class is for non-champion dogs 6 months old or older that were whelped in America from an American breeding.
- Open Class includes any dogs more than 6 months old, including champions.
- Winners Class is open only to this show's undefeated dogs of the same sex that have won first prizes in the Puppy, Twelve-to-Eighteen-Month, Novice, Bred-by-Exhibitor, American-bred, or Open Class. These dogs receive point awards toward their championship. There is an award for the Winners Dog and Winners Bitch.
- Best of Breed or Best of Variety Class is made up of the first-prize recipient from the two Winners Classes (Winners Dog and Winners Bitch) in addition to Champions of Record that are entered for Best of Variety and have been undefeated in any other classes.
- Awards for Best of Opposite Sex to Best of Breed and Best of Variety, and Best of Winners (between Winners Bitch and Winners Dog) are given as well.

In all-breed shows, there are other classes made up of the breeds of each group. There is also a Best in Show award that goes to the best dog in the show, regardless of breed.

Beagle Standard

If you wish to obtain the complete Beagle standard, contact the National Beagle Club or the AKC. (See Useful Addresses and Literature, page 193.) A condensed, paraphrased version of this standard follows.

Beagle varieties are the 13-inch (35-cm), which must not exceed 13 inches in height, and the 15-inch (38-cm), which are over 13 inches tall but not exceeding 15 inches in height

The head is fairly long and broad with ears set moderately low and reaching nearly to the end of her nose when drawn out. Ears are set close to the head with the forward edge slightly inturning to the cheek.

A Beagle's brown or hazel eyes are large, soft, set well apart, and should give her a gentle, pleading expression. Her muzzle is of medium length and square cut. Her lips are free of flews and her nostrils are open and large.

The neck is light, rising freely from shoulders, strong, yet not loaded. Throat is clean and free from skin folds. Shoulders are sloping, clean, and muscular, allowing freedom of action. She should have a deep, broad chest and short back that is strong and muscular. Her well-sprung ribs give her plenty of lung room.

The Beagle's forelegs are straight with ample bone. Pasterns are short and straight and feet are close, round, and firm. Hips and thighs are strong and muscled, with plenty of driving power. Stifles are strong and well let-down with hocks that are firm and symmetrical and moderately bent. Back feet are also close and firm.

The slightly curved Beagle tail is set moderately high, carried gaily, but not turned forward over the back. Her coat is close and hard, typical of a hound, and allowed colors are any true hound color (any combination of black, tan, and white). In general, she appears like a miniature Foxhound, one with the wear-and-tear look that typifies stamina and endurance that can last in the chase and enables her to follow her quarry to the death.

Defects and Faults

Beagle's defects include sharp, terrier-like eyes, a snipy muzzle, a Roman nose, or a dish-faced appearance. Other faults are a thick neck, dewlap, a swayed back, flat ribs, bowed legs, knuckled-over knees, crooked legs, cowhocks, or straight hocks. A thin or soft coat and long or rat-like tail are serious faults as well.

United Kennel Club (UKC)

The UKC is the second largest all-breed, purebred dog registry in the United States. This organization was formed in 1898 and registers more than 225,000 dogs of all breeds annually in all 50 states and over a dozen foreign countries. It supports various activities, principally performance and working dog events, and lays claim to being the largest working dog registry in the world. In 1998, more than 5,000 of the 7,500 UKC programs were working events.

UKC Hunting Beagle Bench Show

This carefully structured show awards UKC Championship points only to Hunting Beagles. The program was begun to enable hunters to register their Beagles without having them confused with Beagles developed for conformation shows only or the modern brace field trials. In order to be eligible to enter, your Beagle must have either participated in the hunt portion of the event that same day, or you must show proof of placement in a previous hunt.

Beagles are shown against others of the same age and sex, and are judged by a UKC-licensed Bench Show Judge. The UKC Beagle standard is assigned a point system that corresponds to the anatomy of the dog. These points add up to 100. The winners are selected based on the number of points they score out of the perfect 100.

Chapter Thirteen
What's for Dinner?

Dog food. That's the key to Sam's nutrition, but have you seen the hundreds of different types, brands, qualities, and prices of this commodity? It's mind boggling! Which one to choose? What percent protein is best? Do all dogs need meat supplements or vitamin additions to maintain good health? How about starches and fats; are they the cause of obese Beagles? What foods should be avoided? When should Sam's diet be increased or decreased?

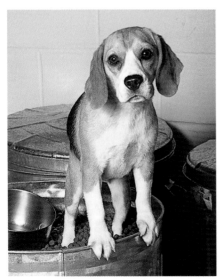

"I finally found the mother-lode!"

Water

An important part of Sam's diet is water. Performance dogs work better when they are properly hydrated. Always carry a supply of water that Sam is accustomed to drinking, whether on a walk or participating in a performance event. Carry his stainless steel water bowl as well, because Beagles don't drink very efficiently from Styrofoam cups.

Free-choice Feeding

Beagles, like most hounds, are often ravenous, even gluttonous, eaters and can rarely be fed free-choice. That term refers to the practice of leaving a quantity of dry food in a self-feeder for Sam's occasional snacking, a method often advantageous for dogs with less voracious appetites.

If you wish to try free-choice feeding, begin when Sam is still a puppy and is no more interested in food than play. If you see that he eats a few mouthfuls and leaves the rest for later, the free-choice plan might work. Frequent small meals often are better for the average dog than one or two larger meals.

Feeding Frequency

When Sam joins your family, feed him exactly as the breeder indicated in the puppy's dietary information. Use the same food, given at the same frequency, and in the same quantities. After a few days, he will become acclimated to your home and routine, and you can make changes, but do so slowly.

At the pet store or supermarket, you'll get about what you pay for. Beagles are small dogs, and the best food available should be affordable. If Sam was being fed a questionable product and you wish to change his diet, buy a premium-quality dry food. Any time you make diet changes, do so gradually, mixing first one-quarter new food, three-quarters old food. After a few days, mix new with old half and half, and so forth.

You can combine his dry food with a premium canned food, but it isn't necessary. Add a bit of warm water to the dry food and wait for a few seconds until it becomes saturated.

Feed Sam premium puppy food, three times daily until he's six months old, and twice daily from six months to a year. At a year of age, his diet can be changed to a premium adult ration.

Continue feeding Sam twice daily, regardless of the manufacturer's recommendations. During intensive schooling periods, or when he's working hard, accommodate for these stresses by increasing the quantities of food offered in each meal.

From an early age, Sam should be weighed periodically. While still a growing puppy and anytime he is under stress conditions, weigh him weekly. If he fails to maintain a normal growth pattern or if he begins to lose weight when working, increase the quantity of his meals slightly until his weight stabilizes.

Accordingly, if Sam begins to look a bit pudgy and his weight is climbing, decrease the quantity of each meal until his weight stabilizes, then maintain that quantity and continue to check his weight regularly.

Feeding Cost

Unfortunately, there are many dog foods available that will keep Sam alive but won't give him the best nutrition available. We are what we eat. Sam will eat what you put in his bowl regardless of its nutritional quality. He won't complain much about the taste of poor food, but his health will suffer. He'll look okay but won't have that extra sheen to his coat. He may be more vulnerable to illness on a get-by diet, and his attitude may not be as agreeable as you might wish.

Stay away from products that have low shelf turnover in the store, and don't buy excessive quantities at one time. If Sam is the only dog on your shopping list, remember he only weighs 18 pounds (8 kg), so don't buy his food in 50-pound (22-kg) bags. By the time he gets to the bottom of the bag, its nutritional content may have decreased significantly. Antioxidant stabilizers have been added to the food, but they aren't perfect. Deterioration rate is increased when food is exposed to heat and room air and fat may become rancid; vitamins A, D, E, and K deteriorate, and B complex may be lost.

Nutritional Terms

Definitions of a few terms will aid in understanding canine nutrition.

The National Research Council (NRC) of the National Academy of Sciences reviews scientific data and establishes the minimum nutritional requirements of dogs of all ages, under varying circumstances.

The American Association of Feed Control Officials (AAFCO) is the agency that regulates dog food label statements, such as *complete and balanced*, which is the AAFCO designation for a food that lacks no nutrients according to feeding trials.

Anabolism is the process by which Sam changes food into living tissue, and *catabolism* is the process by which that tissue is changed into energy and waste products. *Metabolism* refers to the combination of these biological processes and is used to describe the constant physical processes going on within the body of a live being by which foods are digested and used to produce energy and tissue renewal.

Bioavailability refers to the amount of a food ingredient actually used for energy. A dog food containing elements that are not digested may offer a colorful label but it falls short of good nutrition.

Energy Required

Active dogs need more energy than couch potatoes. On a nutrition per pound of body weight basis, growing puppies require twice the nutrition of adults. Little dogs need more calories per pound than big ones. It follows that a growing, active Beagle pup is at the top of this pyramid. So how do you select the best food for Sam?

Weight, feel, and appearance are the best indicators of good nutrition. Feel Sam's barrel (chest); if his ribs are felt but not seen, that's good. If his coat is shiny and his skin is supple and moveable due to a thin fat cover over his skeleton, that's an excellent indictor of good nutrition. If in doubt, a quick trip to Sam's veterinarian should answer the question.

Reading Labels

A dog food label is a legal document that tells you a great deal, providing you know what to look for. Every dog food label must identify its ingredients, which are listed in order

"I prefer table-food, thank you!"

Calories

Energy produced from food when oxidized (digested) in Sam's body is measured in *Kcal,* which is the abbreviation for kilocalories or large calories. Technically, one Kcal is the amount of heat energy required to bring one kilogram of water from 15 to 16°C.

Fat

Fat contains 9 Kcal per gram and is a calorie-dense nutrient containing all essential fatty acids. Fats differ in palatability; those derived from animals usually taste better than those extracted from vegetables, but they contain the same number of calories per gram. Animal or vegetable fats provide adequate fatty acids for your Beagle.

Adult maintenance diets should contain a minimum of 5 percent fat. Slightly more may be desirable to improve the quality of coats or to improve food palatability. Just remember that, in excess, fat is fattening!

Protein

Vegetable protein elements, called amino acids, have lower bioavailability and are less palatable than amino acids of animal origin.

Adult maintenance diets should contain about 18 percent protein, including specific amounts of ten essential amino acids. Amino acid deficiency may result in poor coat, reduced growth rate, condition or weight loss, and in extreme deficiency, death.

of quantity. If soy flour is listed first, the product contains more soy flour than any other ingredient.

A dog food that meets the recommendations of the NRC may apply only to *maintenance* requirements. Such a food is adequate for dogs under minimal stress but is inadequate for growing puppies, performance dogs, or breeding animals.

Labels may specify the *total* quantities of various elements and never mention their *bioavailability*. If in doubt, call or write the manufacturer or select another product.

Read carefully the sources of protein in addition to the quantities.

Excessive quantities of amino acids aren't good either. Protein should always be balanced with the total Kcal of the diet.

Dietary protein of 20 percent generally is sufficient for growing puppies, and 15 percent or less usually is considered too little. Increased protein demands are seen during heavy schooling and work, but these levels gradually decrease as the dog ages. As a senior citizen, Sam will require a higher quality protein in a lowered quantity.

Starch

Calories derived from carbohydrates or starches are often the cause of Beagle obesity. Dogs have a low, almost insignificant, requirement for starches, but some manufacturers use this cheap source of calories to increase the total energy content of their foods.

Minerals

Twelve different essential minerals are required in canine diets. According to the NRC *Nutrient Requirements of Dogs*, to provide the optimal mineral balance, the diet should contain a ratio of 1.2 to 1.4 parts calcium to 1 part phosphorus.

Vitamins

No less than 11 vitamins must be included in canine diets. Vitamin C isn't required because dogs adequately manufacture this element. Vitamin A can be toxic in high doses, and vitamins D and E requirements are interrelated with other nutrients. Requirements and dangers of exces-

sive or insufficient intake are covered in the NRC book mentioned above.

Supplements

It's impossible to feed cheap dog food and hope to cover its inadequacies with vitamin-mineral supplements. *Premium* dry dog foods need no supplementation.

Sam's coat sheen may be improved by adding vegetable or fish oil, lecithin, or fatty acid supplements, but usually these aren't needed when he's fed a premium food diet. Ask Sam's veterinarian about supplements when he's subjected to stresses and always check before using over-the-counter supplements.

Don't feed milk, meat, or eggs, either raw or cooked. Meat supplements such as tripe or liver, and bone meal, were popular in the past, but have been proven unnecessary and sometimes dangerous.

Feeding Trials

Premium brand foods will include on their labels an AAFCO feeding trial statement. These products will contain the right amount of bioavailable food elements for puppies, youths, and working adults, as proven by testing the food in colonies of dogs. If such a statement isn't included on the label, call or write to the manufacturer and ask for feeding trial results.

Dog Food Types

Each type of food has advantages and drawbacks.

Canned

Canned food is the most expensive, but it stores well and is quite palatable.

It may not give Sam adequate vegetable fiber in his diet, and may predispose him to urinary frequency due to the diuretic effect of preservatives and seasoning. Canned food contains about 60 percent water. Meat quality in canned foods may not be the best, and some canned foods contain virtually no meat. Read the label carefully!

Semimoist

Looking like ground meat, semi-moist foods rarely contain any appreciable amount of animal protein.

They don't keep as well as canned foods, cost more per pound, and may contain sugars and chemical preservatives that constitute health risks. Diets of semimoist products may promote excessive water consumption and frequent urination. These foods are sometimes incriminated as the cause of certain allergic reactions as well.

Dry Food

Kibble or dry dog food usually is the least expensive diet and the best for Sam.

All dry foods don't come from the same hopper; they are as different as the dogs that eat them, varying in cost, quality, and palatability.

Premium Quality Foods

Pound for pound the most costly foods available, premium foods are biologically the most economical. The high nutritional content means you feed less quantity; high bioavailability means less waste and smaller volumes of feces produced.

Except to increase palatability, no great advantage is obtained by mixing premium dry foods with canned products. If you do mix one with the other, choose premium, balanced canned foods to mix with premium dry food.

Other Commercial Foods

Favorite brand name dry foods have been around for many years and continue to provide excellent canine nutrition. As you would expect, the quality varies from one product to another. If in doubt, call or write to the manufacturer and ask for the bioavailability of the nutritional elements, feeding trial results, analysis, and the sources of the ingredients.

Generic Brands

The major problem with generic dog foods is their seasonal variation in composition. The law of supply and demand tends to govern the particular commodities that are used in their formulation. If wheat is plentiful, you may find it higher in the formula, and a bumper corn crop will be reflected by an increase in that grain.

Homemade Diets

Formulating Sam's diet in your kitchen is a disservice to him and often leads to nutritional problems. Please leave dog food production to those who have analytical laboratories, research facilities, and feeding trials to test their products.

Readers are referred to the discussion of old dog diseases in Chapter 14, page 153, for further information on this subject and obesity.

Puppy Rations

Formulated especially for growing puppies, puppy foods should furnish adequate nutrition for normal growth and development of young Beagles. Like other rations, you'll get what you pay for.

A label designating the product as *puppy food* doesn't mean you can accept it without question. Quality, sources, and percentages of constituents are critical. Feeding trials are also carried out on puppy food, and the AAFCO label should be found on puppy rations.

Stress Diets

These are the diets formulated specifically for dogs under the

stresses of breeding, whelping, nursing, training, and working. If Sam is under stress, consult his veterinarian for advice prior to investing in a stress diet.

Special Diets

Foods are available by prescription or over the counter to help treat kidney disease, diabetes, gastritis, flatulence, and other health problems. Consult your veterinarian before you use these foods.

"Just one more bite and I'll go. Honest!"

Junk food is no good for Beagles!

Treats

Give pea-sized treats, and as long as Sam isn't receiving more than an ounce or two daily, they're okay. To be sure you're not overfeeding him, measure the quantity of his daily treats, and deduct that amount from his daily ration. If he responds well to his regular dog food, use a bit of that as a training treat. If you buy commercial treats, check the constituents the same as if they were his regular food.

Dietary Aids

Specially constructed devices make feeding interesting for dogs and slow their eating by dispensing dry food one piece at a time. Sam can push the device around his crate, pen, or backyard for an extended period of time to get a meal. These devices are available in most pet supply stores and catalogs.

Human Foods

Generally, it's best to put human food on the dining table and dog food on the floor. This advice isn't arbitrary and, for the record, here are some reasons.

• Milk will usually bring on bouts of diarrhea.

• Meat, especially organ meats (liver, heart, kidney) may cause diarrhea and will upset dietary balance.

• Cooked bones are attractive dietary nuisances. Chicken or chop bones, steak bones, ribs, and some roast bones may splinter when Sam chomps down on them. Bone shards may lodge in his mouth or throat, or they may be swallowed where they can cause other medical mischief.

• Ice cream, candy, pizza, potato chips, peanuts, and a host of other human junk foods are difficult for Sam to digest and should be avoided.

• Table scraps are reported to be the most important cause of pancreatic inflammation, causing damage to that organ's duct system, with sometimes fatal results.

• Chocolate can poison Sam. (For more information about chocolate poisoning and treatment, see page 183.)

Chapter Fourteen

Beagle Health

Health Plan

Being a relatively small dog, a properly cared for Beagle should live for 12 to 15 years. Although Beagles are unique in many respects, their susceptibility and resistance to most infectious diseases are about the same as other hound breeds and indeed the entire canine species.

Diet

The foremost strategy in your Beagle's health maintenance plan is to start with a healthy pup from healthy parents. Throughout Rosy's life, adjust her diet to her needs, and never fail to feed the best quality dog food.

Preventive Medicine

The second most important part of your Beagle's health maintenance plan is preventive medicine. Even if you live in an isolated community, keep Rosy's vaccinations current. Immunizations are critical to the continuation of good health and, although they aren't perfect, these vaccinations are good and improve annually.

Always consult with Rosy's veterinarian at least once a year. Keep a list of questions that occur to you, and when you take her for her annual vaccinations, read them off. In show and performance dogs of all ages and in companion pets after the age of five or six, an annual physical examination is advised.

Preventive medicine might also include neutering or spaying if your Beagle isn't a field trial, show, or breeding prospect. These common canine procedures are among the most important to good health and are discussed further in Chapter 17.

Prompt Treatment of Ailments

Last, but certainly not least important, is prompt attention to Rosy's ailments. This doesn't mean running to her veterinarian with every broken toenail or sneeze. Many of her minor illnesses will run their course and can be handled at home. However, awareness of the signs of serious maladies will help you evaluate when she should be seen by her veterinarian, and when you should apply a Band-Aid or give an aspirin and call the doctor in the morning.

A good veterinarian: Veterinarians shouldn't be branded as good or bad; they are found with various personalities, talents, and practices.

Veterinary practice is a business. Some practices seem to be all business with little compassion for the pet, others seem to lack a desired technical approach, and still others are so specialist-oriented that each patient is subjected to full laboratory screening before examination. Somewhere out there among the thousands of veterinarians who graduate each year is the right one for you.

Instead of reading ads in yellow pages, you should think about what you desire in a veterinarian. Do you want a laid-back general practitioner who takes time to explain things as he examines Rosy, or do you prefer one who exhibits speed and professionalism, and has technicians to complete most of the exam?

The following questions are designed for you to ask potential veterinarians or their staff on the first meeting. It isn't necessary for each question to be answered in the affirmative, but the answers should give you a better understanding of the functions of the clinic.

• Do you take emergency out-of-hours calls?
• If not, to whom are they referred?
• What are your office hours?
• Are appointments required, and if so, how far in advance?
• May I schedule a tour of your hospital?
• Do you have diagnostic laboratory facilities on the premises?

"You won't hurt him, will you doctor?"

- Do you have X-ray and ultrasound equipment?
- Are you equipped for gastroscopic exams?
- What are your paying or billing requirements?
- Do you recommend pet insurance?
- Do you publish a fee schedule? May I have one?
- If not, what is the fee for a routine office call?
- How much will you charge to spay (castrate) my Beagle?
- What is the annual cost for flea and tick control?
- What vaccinations do you recommend for Rosy?
- How often should I have Rosy checked for worms?

Puppy Illnesses

This discussion describes simple illnesses, their signs, and their treatment. If quick recovery isn't seen, consult Rosy's veterinarian immediately.

Potential Poisoning

Each time Rosy opens a cupboard door, it's possible for her to be poisoned. When such an event takes place, before you close the door, look inside and try to ascertain what objects or chemicals may have been swallowed. If any open bottles or spilled contents are seen, carefully read the labels, contact your veterinarian, and watch Rosy for signs of illness, such as lethargy, vomiting, or diarrhea.

Diarrhea

Unformed or liquid feces is common to all pups. Diarrhea is the hallmark of digestive problems; it may be a sign (symptom) of an intestinal irritation. Diarrhea often results when Rosy overeats or consumes the wrong foods. Rich foods such as milk or table scraps usually are to blame. Rosy may continue to display normal appetite and activity, but her bowel control is faulty, and her feces are watery.

When diarrhea is first noticed, withhold all food. Allow modest amounts of drinking water, but feed nothing for 12 hours, and keep her confined for observation. A small pen on the porch or a bathroom with the floor covered with newspapers will do. During her confinement, watch for lethargy, vomiting, bloody stool, or other signs of serious illness.

If none of these signs are seen by the end of the 12-hour fast, start her on a diet of one part cooked rice, one part dry, fat-free cottage cheese, and one part cooked and drained hamburger. Mix these ingredients together and give her about one-third the total daily quantity of food she is accustomed to, divided into three meals. Feed no other food for at least two days. Tofu or tapioca may be used instead of cooked rice.

If her problem is simply from eating something indigestible, a day or two of this bland diet should be sufficient. While on the bland diet, administer orally either Kaopectate or bismuth subsalicylate (Pepto Bismol)

"Let's see—what's in here?"

three times daily. Call your veterinarian for the dosage for your Beagle's age and size.

If diarrhea persists, is bloody, or is accompanied by vomiting, hasten to her veterinarian.

Vomiting

Vomiting also isn't a disease but rather a sign of stomach or small intestine irritation.

Immediate veterinary assistance should be sought when blood is seen in Rosy's vomitus or when it contains bits of sponge rubber, shreds of steel wool, or any other foreign material.

Beagle puppies may eat anything. Compost, leaves, sticks, bones, pieces of toys, leaves, or grass may cause vomiting, sometimes accompanied by diarrhea. Confinement is a necessary part of treatment. Withhold all food and water for 24 hours and watch for blood in the vomit or diarrhea.

Give nothing orally to a vomiting dog. If vomiting has subsided or stopped within four hours, allow Rosy to lick a couple of ice cubes and watch her closely thereafter. If vomiting doesn't resume, administer bismuth subsalicylate three times daily. After a 24-hour fast, feed the aforementioned bland diet concurrently with the oral medication. Boil rice in an overabundance of water, then chill the water and allow Rosy to drink it.

If the bland diet seems to correct the problem, continue to feed it for three days, then gradually mix her regular diet with it.

Scratching

Rosy will occasionally scratch at her body. Ignore it if the scratching is intermittent and infrequent. If itching persists, it may be a sign of flea infestation, mange mites, dry skin, allergy, or other disease and should initiate a trip to your veterinarian.

If Rosy scratches an ear, it might be evidence of ear mites or an ear infection. Biting at the skin just above her tail may indicate overfull or impacted anal sacs, and chewing at one foot could be caused by a sliver, a cactus thorn, or a pad injury.

Appropriate treatment depends on the cause of Rosy's scratching. If fleas are seen, buy a bottle of flea shampoo and follow label directions. (Flea control is discussed on page 170.)

If the cause of Rosy's scratching is not apparent, her veterinarian will be able to diagnose the condition and prescribe treatment.

Preventable Diseases

Most Beagle breeders begin a series of vaccinations soon after puppies are weaned, and annual booster vaccinations should be continued throughout Rosy's life. Her vaccination schedule must be tailored to meet her particular needs, including projected travel, hunting or showing activities, and the locale or region of the country where you live. Only you and your veterinarian can formulate Rosy's vaccination schedule.

Canine Distemper (CD)

The Beagle is reported to have a hereditary predisposition to Canine Distemper, which is occasionally called Dog Plague or Hard Pad. Caused by a virus that attacks the dog's brain, and respiratory and intestinal tracts, this disease is a puppy killer. CD reservoirs exist in stray dog populations and wild animals, such as coyotes, raccoons, foxes, and mink.

Infected weanling puppies often die without displaying visible signs. Older dogs show various signs, such as coughing, fever, appetite loss, lethargy, dehydration, diarrhea, and vomiting. Yellow or green discharge often is seen exuding from the eyes of affected dogs. Hardened footpads, tooth enamel deficiencies, and permanent neurological signs, such as blindness or twitching of extremities, may affect surviving dogs. A few dogs seem to respond to various treatments, only to die later from convulsions and paralysis.

The first of a series of CD vaccinations given at weaning time may be combined with other vaccines, and annual boosters are required. If traveling extensively and mixing with strange dogs, Rosy's exposure potential is increased; consult with her veterinarian about more frequent vaccinations.

Infectious Canine Hepatitis (ICH or CAV-1)

Another contagious, incurable disease, CAV-1 causes sometimes fatal damage to the liver. It is highly communicable among dogs, but is not contagious to humans. CAV-1 is an abbreviation for the causative organism, Canine Adenovirus, type 1.

Signs often mimic those of distemper, and affected puppies often die quickly.

Vaccines are highly effective in preventing CAV-1 and usually are combined with other vaccines at weaning time; annual boosters are required.

Leptospirosis

Usually shortened to *Lepto,* this disease causes kidney damage that may be fatal. Lepto may infect humans as well as other mammals, is quite contagious, and is transmitted by urine. Often, the reservoir for this disease is aquatic rodents.

Signs of Lepto include lethargy, appetite loss, thirst, rusty-colored urine, diarrhea, and vomiting. Affected dogs sometimes walk with a peculiar stilted, roach-backed gait. Antibiotic treatment may be effective, but permanent kidney damage often results from Lepto. Vaccine usually is combined with CD and CAV-1 vaccines at weaning time and is repeated annually.

Parvo and Corona Viruses

Both diseases typically produce severe diarrhea, vomiting, dehydration, and depression. Spread by saliva, feces, vomit, or one-on-one contact with affected dogs, these diseases often are puppy killers. Humans may spread the causative virus on shoes or clothes.

Vaccinations usually are given at about weaning age, and annual boosters are required. Consult with your veterinary practitioner about the

use of these products and the age at which they should be given.

Kennel Cough

This syndrome is caused by a variety of viruses and bacteria working together to produce coughing, fever, loss of appetite, and depression. Principal causative organisms are *Parainfluenza* virus and *Bordetella* bacteria. Uncomplicated, it may cause coughing for two or three weeks, and if accompanied by pneumonia, the syndrome may be fatal. Dogs of all ages are susceptible, but puppies often are worst affected.

Kennel cough is quite contagious and is easily spread by airborne droplets of saliva and nasal discharge from an affected dog's cough or sneeze.

Vaccines for this syndrome include intranasal types that are often less predictable than injectable types, but their reliability has improved. Consult with your veterinarian about the best product, especially when boarding Rosy or entering her in any event where she will contact other dogs.

Lyme Disease

The common deer tick is the vector of this dog and human disease. Lyme disease now exists in at least 40 states. White-tailed deer and field mice are the principal reservoir hosts for the Lyme virus.

Fever, lameness, pain, swelling, and heat in leg joints are some signs of this disease. Effective treatment depends on early diagnosis.

The risk of Lyme disease is related to the length of time an infected tick is attached to Rosy. When in an area where deer ticks are known to exist, check her daily. The tiny black or red-and-black deer tick measures about 0.1 inch (0.4 cm) and resembles a little mole on the skin. The tick sucks blood and grows much larger, with the female tick reaching the size of a grape. (Follow the directions on page 171 for tick removal.)

A Lyme disease vaccine is available, but its efficacy has been questioned. Newly developed vaccines may prove more effective, and tick control programs are essential.

Her itch is caused by an allergy.

Rabies

Rabies, a fatal viral disease of all warm-blooded animals, including dogs and humans, is spread primarily by contact with the saliva of an infected animal and usually is associated with bite wounds.

Rabies vaccines are excellent, but the disease is far from under control. The U.S. Centers for Disease Control and Prevention reported 5,751 cases of rabies in wild and domestic animals between January 1 and October 31, 1998; no human infections were reported.

Brain changes are the principal signs of rabies. The disease takes from two weeks to several months to develop. The virus travels from the bite location to the brain by way of nerve trunks. Therefore, if the infecting bite occurs on a hind foot, it results in a long incubation period.

After reaching the brain, the virus migrates to the salivary glands.

Signs of rabies vary from aggressiveness and irritability to paralysis, producing furious or dumb rabies.

Reservoirs for rabies virus are found in wild animals, such as skunks, foxes, raccoons, coyotes, bats, and other wildlife. This incurable and often fatal disease can infect all warm-blooded animals. Therefore, great emphasis is placed on rabies vaccination programs.

Rabies vaccine usually is administered later than other vaccines. Check with Rosy's veterinarian for local requirements.

Diseases Without Vaccinations

Many diseases have no vaccines or prevention programs. Beaglers should be aware of these conditions and consult a veterinarian if they are encountered.

Allergies

Allergies take the form of skin redness, stomach upsets, itching, or joint and muscle pain. Common canine allergies are associated with flea saliva, milk products, and irritating plants such as poison ivy or nettles. Rosy may become allergic to various medications, parasites, or inhaled dusts or pollens.

Sometimes signs of allergy are vague and defy easy diagnosis. Motivated owners should note changes in their Beagle, and, if Rosy displays strange signs of illness, record their occurrence relative to

Routine physical exams are part of preventive medicine.

walks, meals, sleep, and weather. Call your veterinarian and describe what you've observed.

Otitis Externa (Ear Infection)

Wax buildup in the external ear canal predisposes to a secondary infection. Itch associated with the wax causes Rosy to scratch violently, which in turn causes serum to ooze into the canal, which feeds the infecting bacteria. Therapy includes thorough cleaning and medication placed into the ear canal by Rosy's veterinarian.

Beagles and other long-eared dogs are at risk for foreign material in their ear canals. Seedpods of some wild grasses are called awns. They are small pointed structures that are attached to stiff beards. You may have picked these bristly little nuisances from your socks after a trip to the country. Those same bearded awns often make their way into Beagle ear canals causing great discomfort and necessitating a trip to Rosy's veterinarian for removal.

Ear Hematoma

Ear hematoma often accompanies other ear diseases. The condition looks like a fat ear and results from Rosy shaking her head, whipping her long ears. Vessels are broken within the ear flap, and a pocket of blood forms between layers of ear cartilage and skin.

Rosy's veterinarian will first treat the causative otitis, then drain the blood serum and obliterate the pocket, usually by surgical means. The ear is immobilized by bandage, and healing is usually uncomplicated.

Eartip Wounds

Appearing like tiny scissor snips, these wounds are quite irritating and often are complicated by flies that suck serum from the wounds. These wounds are the result of long ears dragging though the brush or whipping in the wind behind Rosy when she is on trail.

Usually, the condition can be treated with cauterization, sometimes followed with bandaging. Occasionally the tip of the ear must be surgically trimmed to remove scar tissue that complicates healing. Sometimes Rosy's ears must be placed in a loose stocking-like snood when she runs. Uninformed owners often ignore tiny lacerations, much to the discomfort of the Beagle.

Prostatitis

This is an adult intact male dog disease. The signs of this condition are difficult urination, stiff gait, fever, loss of appetite, and a foul discharge from the penis. Prostatitis should never be ignored. It may be treated with antibiotics, or castration may be advised. Untreated, it could result in a systemic infection that could be fatal.

Ehrlichiosis

Ehrlichiosis is transmitted by the brown dog tick and is manifested by nosebleeds, swelling of the legs, anemia, and a multitude of other signs. If not treated early, it can be

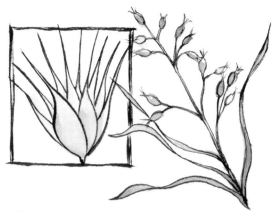

Grass awns are frequently the cause of otitis.

fatal. Although no vaccine is available, tick control is an important means of prevention.

Hereditary Diseases

More than 300 different genetic diseases are recognized in present-day canines, but DNA testing is diagnostic for less than 20. Most hereditary diseases follow certain bloodlines and can be controlled by selective breeding.

Eye Conditions

Beagle eye problems are sometimes hereditary, but others are the result of aging. Some genetic eye conditions, such as ectropion, are related to the loose skin of the face, which occurs in a few Beagles. The breed occasionally is afflicted with primary glaucoma, prolapse of the third eyelid-gland, cataract, cataract with microphthalmia, ectasia syndrome, progressive retinal atrophy, and hereditary tapetal degeneration.

Progressive retinal atrophy: Progressive retinal atrophy (PRA) is a serious hereditary eye disease. During the progress of the disease, a degeneration of retinal cells occurs, which leaves the dog unable to see stationary objects. In Beagles, PRA usually causes vision impairment by about five years of age, when dilated pupils and night blindness are noticed.

Beagle brood stock should be examined for this disease. Ask your veterinarian about the various certifying agencies such as the Canine Eye Registry Foundation (CERF). Some affected dogs are treated, but a cure for PRA is unlikely. If her vision diminishes slowly, Rosy will adapt to her blindness and live a normal life span as a pet.

Cherry eye: The nictitating membrane, also called the third eyelid,

usually appears as a tiny pink structure located at the inside corner (nasal canthus) of the eye. The gland located on the underside of that membrane sometimes becomes inflamed and swollen, causing the entire third eyelid to turn inside out. This results in a horrible-appearing red mass, which doesn't seem to bother the dog at all.

Cherry eye is easily diagnosed and can be treated either by surgically removing the gland, surgically tacking it in place, or sometimes by medication to combat the swelling and infection. A predisposition for cherry eye can be inherited.

Cataracts: Cataract is opacity within the lens, which lies immediately behind the iris. In the Beagle's hereditary cataract, the lens lesion usually is seen in the rear portion of the lens of the left eye. Cataract with microphthalmia is a specific genetic disease wherein the affected Beagle is born with very small eyes, opaque lenses, and retinal folds.

Primary glaucoma: Glaucoma occurs when the fluid pressure within the eyeball increases, causing significant discomfort and possibly damage to other ocular structures followed by blindness. The condition is diagnosed with special instruments and is treated both medically and surgically with reasonable success. This genetic disease of the Beagle is accompanied by lens dislocation and is transmitted as a recessive trait.

Beagle hereditary tapetal degeneration and ectasia syndrome are

Typical appearance of cherry eye.

genetic conditions of the retina and its related structures. These diseases currently are receiving more attention by ocular research organizations.

Skeletal Conditions

Very few hereditary limb conditions exist in the Beagle, probably because of the propensity of breeders to propagate for soundness.

Canine hip dysplasia (CHD): This common hereditary disease of many purebred dogs is nearly unknown in the Beagle, and only one breeder was contacted who reported seeing CHD in Beagles. However, the disease is quite prevalent in dozens of other purebreds, including many that are smaller in stature than the Beagle.

CHD is a genetic developmental disease. The Orthopedic Foundation for Animals (OFA) researchers believe that all dogs are born with normal hips, and the radiographic (X ray) signs of CHD begin to show up at several months to several years of age. Their records indicate that 95 percent of all dysplastic dogs can be diagnosed by pelvic X ray by 24 months of age.

Although dozens of techniques are used to help dysplastic dogs, no cure is possible for this deformity. Selective breeding of dogs two or more years old, which have OFA-certified normal hips, has lowered the incidence remarkably.

CHD has been around a long time and is known to be hereditary, but the exact mechanism of transmission is not clear. A few old wives' tales should probably be shot down any-

Senior citizens often have unrecognized needs.

way. These excerpts are taken from the OFA description of CHD.

• No scientific evidence exists to show any vitamin or mineral supplement will prevent CHD or reduce its effects.

• CHD can't be caused by high caloric intake and rapid growth.

• Exercise, jumping, and slick floors do not cause CHD.

• Injuries to the pelvic area are easily differentiated from CHD.

• No environmental factors can cause CHD.

Multiple epiphyseal dysplasia: This is a recessive disease of Beagle puppies in which the hind leg joints sag, causing a swaying gait in the pup's hindquarters. It is associated with defective bone formation.

Intervertebral disk disease: This crippling genetic condition is probably associated with exaggerated conformation and is reported by a number of Beagle breeders. It will likely appear at middle age and causes intense pain, especially in the neck region when moving or being handled.

This disease is seen when the cushioning disks between spinal bones dislocate or rupture, exerting pressure on the spinal cord. The position of the disk injury determines the severity of signs displayed. Signs are intense pain, shaking, or general discomfort with or without paralysis of the hind legs. It may occur suddenly and progress to total posterior paralysis within a short time, or it may leave the Beagle with the ability to walk unsteadily, weaving and staggering.

This disease must receive immediate professional diagnosis and therapy.

Dwarfism: The hereditary disease called *chondrodystrophy* or dwarfism is a bane to several unrelated breeds, including the Alaskan Malamute and the Beagle. Simply put, it involves a growth defect in the long bones of the legs, which leaves the Beagle with a stunted appearance. Signs of the deformity are usually exhibited by three or four weeks of age, and some puppies suffer pain during that time. If the dwarf Beagle matures, she may have a normal life span, but will probably be inactive.

X rays of the legs and spine will diagnose the disease between three weeks and three months of age. There is evidence that the dwarf syndrome may include deformities or absence of nasal sinuses as well. Many Beagle dwarfs are euthanized before weaning, when the deformity becomes visibly apparent.

Other Genetic Diseases

Many other named hereditary problems are reported in Beagles, such as short or broken tails, missing or shortened toes, cleft palates and upper lips, and hypothyroidism.

Less common genetic diseases include pulmonic stenosis, a major vessel narrowing at its origin within the chest. Kidney deformities or absence of a kidney is another genetic Beagle disease, and a red blood cell deficiency wherein the cell's life is shortened is another, more rare possibility.

Monorchidism: Beagles are occasionally afflicted with this genetic problem in which the male has only one testicle descended into his scrotum. At birth, both testicles are positioned in the abdomen but by 30 to 40 days of age, both testicles should descend into the scrotum. Testicular retention is hereditary, but the exact genetic mechanism is poorly understood. Retained testicles often develop malignant tumors.

Monorchid males are able to breed, are fertile, and should be castrated before puberty.

Cryptorchidism: Cryptorchids are males with both testicles retained in the abdomen. They will mount and copulate with females, but are unable to produce offspring. Cryptorchid Beagles should be castrated before reaching puberty to prevent development of malignant tumors later in life.

Epilepsy: This condition is reported regularly in Beagles. A seizure disorder said to be inherited in many cases, epilepsy may also result from injury, tumors, or infections. Hereditary epilepsy seizures usually don't begin until the Beagle is more than one year old but may be detected by an electroencephalogram (EEG) at an earlier age.

Epileptic seizures are often brief, and the Beagle returns to normal within a few minutes. Veterinarians usually diagnose the condition by owners' reports, but in some cases, the seizure lasts long enough for the Beagle to make the trip to a veterinarian. The condition is usually treatable with daily medication. No cure is recognized, and untreated, the seizures may become more frequent and more severe and eventually cause death.

Old Dog Diseases

Among these conditions are several diseases of unspayed bitches. Menopause does not occur in female canines. By about six years of age, a bitch has passed her reproductive peak, although she continues to cycle and exhibit normal heat periods. Reproductive problems and Rosy's health risks are likely to increase with each passing year.

Ovariohysterectomy is the best insurance policy you can buy for Rosy.

Metritis and Pyometra

These two infectious uterine diseases affect unspayed bitches. Metritis is occasionally fatal in young and middle-aged females, and pyometra is an extremely dangerous type of metritis. In both diseases, risk is greatly increased with age, and both can be averted by ovariohysterectomy.

Mammary Tumors

Breast tumors account for nearly half of all canine tumor cases, and at least half of all breast tumors are

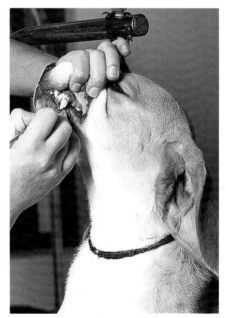

Dental exams and tartar scaling are extremely important.

malignant. They may occur at any age, but are more common in intact females past six years old. If spayed at or before puberty, the risk of mammary tumors is negligible, but each time Rosy comes in heat, her predisposition for these tumors increases.

Arthritis

Hip joints are most commonly affected, but in an aging Beagle, virtually every joint is subject to the pain of arthritis.

Your veterinarian can best advise you of proper treatment for arthritis. Nonsteroidal anti-inflammatory drugs (NSAIDs), such as ibuprofen and buffered aspirin, may be of value. Acetaminophen may be used to dispel pain. Old dogs' digestive tracts are somewhat sensitive, and *no drug should be used without first calling your veterinarian.*

Lick Granuloma

Rosy compulsively begins to lick and chew at an easily accessible extremity, such as a wrist, toe, or lower leg. Granuloma is the rounded, pink, fleshy tissue mass growing within such an abrasion. Lick lesions may be initiated by anything that irritates and attracts her attention to a certain area and usually are associated with flea bites, bee stings, tiny cuts, slivers, or painful arthritic joints.

A vicious cycle begins. The spot itches, so Rosy licks and chews. The more she licks, the worse the lesion becomes until the cycle is habitual. Veterinary care should be sought immediately when compulsive licking begins.

An Elizabethan collar may be worn as a restraint to physically prevent licking. Sometimes, the collar is combined with topical antibiotics or steroids to relieve surface infection and combat the itch. Occasionally, tricyclic antidepressants or opiate blockers may help.

Skin Cysts and Tumors

Old Beagles often develop benign wart-like tumors and skin cysts on their faces and legs. Frequently, fatty tumors are found just under the skin of Rosy's abdomen and chest as well. Therapy depends on her age and general health, as well as the size and position of the mass. If Rosy is quite old, and the masses aren't causing her any discomfort, they may be ignored.

Calluses

These usually harmless lesions result from lying on concrete, wood, or other hard surfaces. Calluses are skin thickenings that occur over pressure points, such as elbows, lower legs, and hips. They have no significance unless they become irritated or infected.

Blindness

Nuclear sclerosis refers to clouding of an old dog's lenses and appears much the same as a cataract. It rarely causes total blindness, although vision is no doubt impaired, especially in low-light conditions.

The causes for various old age ocular problems has been assumed to be senility. However, a recent study in dogs indicated more specific causes. Dogs with low plasma levels of vitamin E and vitamin A were found to be particularly affected. This seems to indicate that these deficiencies may be at least partly to blame.

Deficient diets were incriminated, such as those consisting of large quantities of red meat and fat, beef offal, and turkey carcasses, in the absence of commercial dog foods. The high-animal fat diets gave rise to a higher requirement of vitamin E, which led to the deficiency.

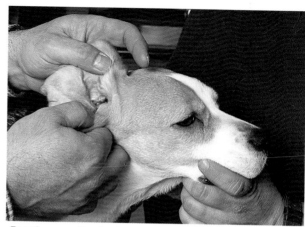
Beagle ears often harbor grass awns that must be removed.

Deafness

Sometimes it's difficult to judge whether a wise old Beagle is actually losing her hearing or is selectively deciding what sounds she'll respond to. In case Rosy is actually losing her hearing, stamp your foot on the floor when you approach her so she won't be surprised by your touch.

Obesity

Obesity is a serious threat to older Beagles and may be an important side effect of several serious metabolic diseases. Even when not associated with a specific underlying disease, obesity will shorten Rosy's life by stressing leg joints and internal organ function and should never be ignored. Schedule an appointment with your veterinarian for a laboratory workup to rule out systemic diseases. If Rosy is simply overweight, begin a careful reducing plan, one that won't cause undue stress.

Use low-calorie dog foods that contain a complete nutritional balance, vitamins, and minerals. With your veterinarian's advice, plan to reduce her weight over a period of months.

Carefully begin an exercise program. Take Rosy for short walks daily or, if possible, several times daily. Months or sometimes years may be added to an obese dog's life by weight reduction and appropriate exercise.

Diabetes

Diabetes mellitus, or sugar diabetes, is a metabolic disease most often seen in older female dogs. Its early signs are lethargy, excessive water consumption, increased urination, and weight gain. Later in the course of the disease, sudden weight loss and vomiting are seen. If you suspect diabetes, consult with Rosy's veterinarian.

Chapter Fifteen

Parasitism

Parasites are organisms that live on or within a living host, causing harm to that host. Canine parasites range from microscopic bacteria, funguses, and mites to visible insects, worms, and other organisms. These parasites may predispose their canine hosts to diseases, and in some cases can cause death.

External Parasites

Canine parasites that live on or within the skin of your Beagle are called ectoparasites. These include fungi, mites, lice, fleas, and ticks. Some over-the-counter medicines for skin conditions may create new problems while doing nothing toward solving the initial one. When you discover a hair loss or skin irritation, invest in a trip to your veterinarian.

Ringworm

Canine ringworm rarely takes the shape of a ring and is not caused by a worm. Ringworm lesions are caused by a microscopic fungus of several different species.

Some ringworm fungi fluoresce when a black light is shined upon them. Others are diagnosed by culturing scrapings taken from infected skin. Microscopic examination of hair roots diagnoses others, but unfortunately, some skin fungi are only diagnosed by ruling out all other causes of skin lesions.

Ringworm fungi are treated by a multitude of medicines, including oral and topical products. Shampoos, lotions, ointments, or tablets may be used to treat ringworm. With patience, practically all cases will eventually respond to treatment.

Mange

Mange is another ectoparasitic condition caused by the invasion of mites, each of which has an individual appearance, life cycle, and its own treatment. Usually, mange-mite infection causes hair loss, skin redness, itching, and irritation.

• *Demodex* is probably the most common mange mite of the Beagle. Demodex mites live in the hair follicles and are most often found in the facial region. Hereditary predisposition to Demodex infection has long been suggested. Many theories are proposed regarding the source of this mite infestation because it doesn't easily spread from one infected dog to another. It may be present in practically all dogs, causing problems when the animal is stressed, and is treatable by nutritional improvement and topical medicines.

• *Cheyletiella,* or the puppy dandruff mite, is seen less regularly and may be diagnosed by microscopic examination of the puppy's dandruff. This mite causes very little trouble and can be eliminated by practically any shampoo.

• *Psoroptes* and *Sarcoptes* mites are sometimes seen in Beagles, but no more often than in other breeds. Infestations of these mites usually cause dramatic signs, because they burrow in deeper layers of the dog's skin and are quite irritating. Scrapings taken from skin lesions usually are diagnostic and treatment consists of dips, medicated baths, and topical medicines.

Mange requires early and thorough treatment and follow-up examinations to be sure it is totally cured. Allergies, nutritional problems, hormonal imbalances, and physical irritations are commonly mistaken for parasitism and are thus mistreated.

Ear Mites

Otodectes, the ear mite, is slightly larger than mange mites and may be suspected when dark wax is discovered exuding from the ear canal. These mites cause severe irritation and result in Sam shaking his head and persistently scratching at his ears.

Diagnosis is made by microscopic examination of Sam's ear wax, and treatment consists of cleaning his ears thoroughly and putting mite-killing medication into his ear canals.

Lice

Pediculosis, or louse infestation, is common in some regions of the country. Visible to the unaided eye, lice are either of the sucking or biting variety.

Diagnosis is made by discovering tiny white nits or louse eggs stuck to hairs of Sam's back, often near his rump. The adult lice may be seen scurrying over his skin, causing him to scratch when they bite or penetrate to suck blood.

When you are sure of the diagnosis, buy a powder or shampoo containing safe insecticides and use it. Be sure all insecticide products are

An assortment of ectoparasites.

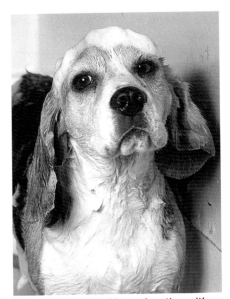
Flea baths are used in conjunction with other programs.

labeled for use on dogs of Sam's age and size.

Fleas

Probably the most irritating canine ectoparasite is also the most common one. The diminutive flea is found on backyard or kenneled Beagles, and heavier infestations are found on those living in warmer, more humid climates. Cat fleas commonly are found on dogs.

Fleas are difficult to treat because they live part of their life cycle off the dog. They create more problems because they are secondary hosts for tapeworms, and the fleas' saliva can cause an allergic reaction in dogs.

Diagnosis is made by running a fine-toothed comb through Sam's coat over his pelvic region. Fleas will be caught between the flea comb's teeth or will jump from his hair to escape the comb. When adult fleas aren't found, you may see some of their excreta (feces), which appear as tiny, black, comma-shaped debris.

Fleas are often responsible for licking, chewing, and scratching, and the formation of hot spots, a related skin condition.

A temporary resident of the dog, the flea hops onto its host, feeds, mates, and lays eggs, which are dropped on Sam's back and fall off in his doghouse or on your carpet. Eggs hatch into larvae that feed on flakes of dandruff and other organic debris. The larvae pupate, adults emerge, and begin looking for a host. The adult flea can live for more than 100 days without a blood meal.

Don't take a flea infestation lightly! Regularly vacuum Sam's doghouse and your carpets, launder his bedding, treat the doghouse and your carpets with dog-safe flea killers, such as Borax powder. This product is nontoxic to dogs and kills fleas by dehydrating them.

If necessary, use a premise spray or flea bomb; carefully follow label directions.

Several new flea products are available from your veterinarian. Some are given orally; others are in liquid form and are applied topically on Sam's skin once a month. Some sterilize flea eggs; others kill adult fleas. Follow your veterinarian's advice about the products, their safety, cost, and effectiveness.

Biological flea control programs are available. One involves application of tiny nematodes (worms) that consume flea eggs but are harmless to humans and pets. Others involve the use of insect growth regulators (IGRs) that interfere with the flea's life cycle.

Organic products such as pyrethrum and other natural insecticides usually are considered safer than chemicals, but are less effective than contemporary manufactured products.

A collar is available that emits high frequency sounds to repel fleas, but its effectiveness is suspect and it doesn't enjoy much consumer acceptance.

Don't use oral medication, dips, sprays, powders, medicated collars, or other drugs that are not labeled for canines of Sam's age and weight. Don't use two products at the same time without approval of your veterinarian. Also be super-careful with systemic medications in a pregnant or lactating female.

Ticks

Ticks bury their heads in their host's skin and suck blood for several days. Male ticks are only about the size of a pinhead; female ticks often reach the size of a grape when they fill with blood. After a blood meal, the female detaches, lays thousands of eggs, then dies. Some ticks complete all their life stages on the dog (as in the brown dog tick), or they may use birds, deer, rodents, or other mammals as secondary hosts.

Ticks are frequently found under Sam's collar, in his armpit region, around his ears, and over his withers.

If you find an embedded tick, put on a pair of rubber gloves and, with tweezers, grasp the insect as close to Sam's skin as possible. Apply firm, steady traction to detach the tick, then kill it by dropping it in a container of rubbing alcohol. Don't try to drown a tick in water, don't squash it, and don't handle it with your bare fingers. (See discussion of Lyme disease on page 158.) If the tick's head breaks off, don't worry; the part of a tick that remains embedded may result in a minor local irritation but rarely causes a systemic infection.

Following tick removal, clean the area once or twice daily with alcohol to keep the scab off and allow drainage from the wound.

Ticks won't detach from Sam's skin if you heat their bodies with the flame of a match or the hot tip of a hair curling iron. Another tick-removal scheme is to place a drop of acetone, alcohol, or nail polish remover on the tick. The rapid evaporation of these products is supposed to make the tick back out quickly. That idea has more credibility than heating the tick, but it doesn't work every time.

Internal Parasites

As the name implies, internal or endoparasites reside inside the Beagle's body.

Nematodes include ascarids (roundworms), kidney worms, spirocerca, and a few others. *Cestodes* are tapeworms and other segmented parasites. Other endoparasites are whipworms, hookworms, and flukes. Protozoa and coccidia are still another type of endoparasites that can seriously affect the general health and vitality of puppies.

Ascarids

Immature roundworms, called larvae, may remain hidden in cysts in a female dog's tissues throughout her life. During pregnancy, the larvae migrate from their cysts into unborn puppy tissues. When the infested pup is born, the larvae migrate into his small intestine, where they mature.

Adult roundworms lay eggs that pass out in the dog's feces and become sources of infestation for other dogs. These and other parasite

ova, or eggs, are identified by microscopic examination of puppies' feces.

Ascarids compete with their host for food and a heavy infestation of roundworms will nearly starve a pup to death. Heavily infested dogs are malnourished, unthrifty, pot-bellied, and lack energy.

A stool sample from Sam should be taken to Sam's veterinarian at least once a year for examination. If roundworm ova are found, the veterinarian will prescribe an appropriate medication for treatment.

Giant Kidney Worm

This somewhat rare nematode, *Dioctophyme renale*, lives in the dog's kidneys. Reaching a yard in length and a half-inch in diameter, these worms lay eggs that are eaten by aquatic worms that look like earthworms. Transfer hosts are either frogs or fish, which eat the aquatic worms, and when dogs eat infested frogs or fish, they become the definitive host. Eggs pass in the infected dog's urine and begin the cycle again.

Spirocerca

Indigenous to the South, this nematode uses dung beetles as secondary hosts. Spirocerca eggs passed by the infected dog are eaten by this beetle, chickens or rodents eat the beetle, then dogs eat infested chicken or rodent carcasses and the life cycle is complete.

After a dog has eaten an infested carcass, the larvae hatch and

Tapeworms are commonly spread by fleas.

Frisbee is this Beagle's bag.

migrate to the dog's esophagus, stomach, or the large chest artery (aorta). The infestation within the dog causes vomiting, coughing, and hemorrhage.

Hookworms

Ancylostoma, the canine hookworm, is another serious parasite that thrives in the South. The egg of this microscopic worm passes in the stool of an infested dog, hatches on the soil, and is capable of penetrating a dog's skin. It then migrates in the tissues, ending up in the small intestine, where the hookworm attaches to the lining of the gut and sucks blood.

The principal signs of hookworms are anemia and gut irritation. The severity of blood loss depends on the degree of infestation; puppies may die from heavy infestations of hookworms.

Diagnosis is made by microscopic examination of a fecal sample. Treatment is usually administered by a veterinarian, and follow-up fecal examinations should be scheduled.

Whipworms

Trichuris infestation is uncommon. This parasite lives in an outpouching of the large intestine, where it causes chronic diarrhea. Diagnosis is made by finding whipworm eggs in fecal examinations. Following aggressive treatment, repeated stool examinations are advised to be sure this parasite is eliminated.

Coccidia

Coccidia are microscopic protozoan parasites that live in a dog's intestine. Usually, infestation (coccidiosis) causes chronic, often bloody diarrhea. Diagnosis is made by fecal examination, and treatment with various medications is usually successful. Repeated fecal examinations are recommended following treatment.

Trypanosoma

Indigenous to the South, this single-cell protozoan endoparasite is transmitted by bug bites. Trypanosomes enter the host's blood and lodge in the heart muscle. Signs of an infestation include pale mucous membranes, lethargy, and sometimes ascites (fluid in the abdomen). There is no known cure for this rare infection.

Heartworms are spread by mosquito bites.

Tapeworms

Requiring secondary hosts, tapeworms aren't transmitted directly from dog to dog. Various species use deer, ground birds, rodents, or fleas as their secondary hosts. A dog must eat part of a carcass of one of these hosts to become infested. Tapeworms compete with their host for food, and a heavily infested dog will appear unthrifty and thin, with a dry coat.

The tapeworm head (scolex) attaches to the lining of the host's intestine, and its segmented body grows to enormous lengths. Diagnosis isn't made by examination of a stool sample, but rather by finding a tiny, white segment attached to hair around the dog's anus or on the surface of his stool.

Killing the tapeworm is only half the treatment because controlling the dog's consumption of host material is equally important. This means controlling the flea population and preventing Sam from eating roadkill deer, rabbits, or other rodents.

Treating Worms

Worm medications are poisons. Beagle owners should rely on their veterinarian to prescribe worm treatment. When medication is prescribed or dispensed by your veterinarian, carefully calculate the dosage and administer the medication according to label directions.

Keep your pup healthy and active by having it treated for worms.

An especially perilous procedure is to treat all puppies for worms, whether or not a parasite infestation is diagnosed. If Sam isn't harboring parasites, don't treat him.

There is no excuse for doing something well that should never be done at all.

Heartworm

In recent years, this parasitic disease has spread to nearly every part of the United States, including arid Arizona and chilly Alaska.

A heartworm larva (*Dirofilaria*) requires transmission by a mosquito, wherein the larva develops for a couple of weeks and is then injected into another dog. The heartworm larva matures into an adult that may reach a foot in length and the diameter of a matchstick. Adult heartworms live in the heart and nearby major arteries. Dynamic heart failure signs are seen with a heavy infestation, and an infected dog acts as a reservoir of infection for other dogs.

Before a preventive program can be initiated, a blood test must show that there are no larvae circulating in Sam's bloodstream. Heartworm prevention is accomplished by means of regular oral medication that is administered at home.

Chapter Sixteen
Beagle Emergencies

Crisis conditions include injuries, wounds, poisoning, and rapidly progressing diseases. Life-threatening emergencies are rarely seen in Beagles that are confined to a backyard, but when the security of a fence is forsaken and Rosy is exploring the great outdoors, a multitude of crisis situations may arise.

First-aid Kit

Every dog owner should carry a canine first-aid kit when taking a dog from its home environs.

Your first-aid kit should include:
• A cell phone, if available. Write Rosy's veterinarian's number down and carry it with you as well, because 911 won't put you directly in touch with canine emergency personnel.
• A tube of antibiotic cream
• Bandage roll, three-inch gauze
• Eyewash, bottle of artificial tears to flush eyes
• Disinfectant, 3-percent hydrogen peroxide solution
• Muzzle, 4-foot length of soft cotton rope
• Pad and pencil

• Scissors with straight blunt tips, or specially made bandage scissors
• Liquid soap for cleaning skin wounds
• Styptic stick, for minor nail bleeding
• Tape, roll of 1-inch
• Thermometer, electronic or mercury-rectal
• Tourniquet, or rubber tube
• Tweezers, or inexpensive hemostatic forceps
• Vital signs chart

These items should fit into a small nylon web belt pack that can be carried with you.

Personal Training

Be prepared for crises in Rosy's life; enroll in a first-aid course for dog owners. Learn various first-aid techniques, proper bandaging procedures, as well as CPR and canine artificial respiration. Learn how to rig a muzzle, apply pressure bandages and tourniquets, and the proper way to carry Rosy when she has suffered an accident or serious injury.

A first-aid course will teach you to count Rosy's respiratory and pulse rates and judge their character.

Is this Beagle practicing a dog walk by herself?

Vital Signs

Normal values

Pulse rate	70 to 90 per minute
Pulse character	Strong and steady
Temperature	101.5°F (38.5°C)
Respiration	10 to 30 per minute
Respiratory character	Even and deep
Mucous membranes	Bright pink, moist
Capillary filling time	2 seconds
Eyes	Bright, corneas clear and moist

Rosy's Normal Values

At rest   *After exercise*

At rest		After exercise
_____	Pulse rate	_____
_____	Pulse quality	_____
_____	Temperature	_____
_____	Respiratory rate	_____
_____	Respiratory character	_____
_____	Mucous membrane	_____
_____	Capillary filling time	_____
_____	Eye appearance	_____

You'll learn how to recognize normal and abnormal mucous membrane colors. Taking her body temperature, capillary filling time, and other vital signs is taught as well.

Vital Signs

When the course is finished, record Rosy's normal vital signs. A sample chart is furnished on page 177; fill in the blanks and put it in your first-aid kit.

Take and record her rectal temperature early one morning, and again after she has been exercising hard. The normal range is from 101.5 to 102.5°F (38.5–39.5°C).

Before and after exercise, record her respiratory rate and the character of her breathing. A dog's normal respiration rate is between 10 and 30 breaths per minute and can only be evaluated when she is breathing through her nose, not while she is panting.

While resting and after heavy exercise, take her pulse by pressing your finger against the inside of her thigh, about half way between her stifle and hip. A Beagle's normal resting heart rate is between 70 and 90 beats per minute. In first-aid class you will learn to differentiate a thin or thready pulse from a strong or bounding pulse.

The color of Rosy's tongue and gums should be a bright, moist pink. Now press your finger tightly against her gums for a few seconds. The mucous membrane will turn white under your finger, and as you remove your finger it will quickly return to its normal color. The time the white area takes to reach the normal pink color is called *capillary filling time*, which should be about two seconds.

Observe Rosy's eyes. They should be bright, moist, and glossy, with crystal clear corneas.

Evaluate First

When you discover that Rosy has been injured, observe her carefully before you touch her. Look for bleeding wounds, legs that aren't normally positioned, eyes that aren't focused or have a blank appearance. Then rapidly formulate a plan to treat her. Prepare to transfer her to an animal hospital as soon as possible. However, without a thorough visual exam, you won't know how to pick her up or hold and carry her.

Muzzle

The most gentle Beagle may snap or bite viciously when in shock, frightened, or in pain. When faced with a personal crisis, Rosy will need your reassurance. Keep your voice calm; speak in low, soothing tones. Approach her slowly at her level; extend your hand, but don't grab at her. Avoid direct eye contact with her and if she shows fear, apply a muzzle before you proceed. Remember, time is important and helping her means handling her.

Tie a loose single knot in the center of the muzzle cord and slip the loop over her closed jaws. Pull the knot snugly on top of her muzzle immediately forward of the stop. Take the ends of the cord beneath her lower jaw and tie another single knot, then wrap both ends of the cord behind her ears and tie a slip-knot. If you don't have a muzzle cord in your first-aid kit, tear a strip of gauze bandage about 4 feet long from a bandage roll, twist it, and substitute it for the cord.

Car Accidents

Beagles love to follow trails, and some trails cross roads. When a 20-pound (9-kg) dog has been hit by a ton of steel, an emergency exists. If a car hits Rosy, you must act quickly to determine whether your best course is an immediate trip to the veterinarian, or, first, treatment at the accident scene to control hemorrhage.

Telephone Rosy's veterinarian, tell him who you are, that your Beagle has been struck by a car, and that you are en route to the clinic.

Control any visible hemorrhage with pressure bandages, then wrap her up; keep her quiet and warm. Use a board, jacket, or blanket as a stretcher on which to transport Rosy. Time is of the essence!

A car accident might result in shock, fractured bones, lacerations, and/or hemorrhage. Of those, shock is the most perplexing.

Recognizing Shock

Shock is a difficult syndrome to define, evaluate, and treat. It's a

If in doubt, muzzle your Beagle.

complex multisymptom condition, one for which you must always be on the alert when emergencies arise. Dogs in shock don't always look the same. They may be unconscious or alert, anxious or depressed, feverish or cold.

Common signs of shock include pale or bluish gums and tongue; prolonged capillary filling time; rapid, shallow respiration; weak, thready pulse; and a rapid heart rate.

Shock may be the result of an incident causing internal or external hemorrhage, or blunt trauma, as well as severe animal bites, poisoning, puncture wounds, or snakebites. Shock also has been seen in cases of acute allergic reaction to antibiotics and other drugs.

Shock may be progressive. When suspected, control bleeding, keep Rosy warm, and get her to a veterinarian quickly.

Artificial Respiration

Canine artificial respiration is simple. With a piece of gauze wrapped around your finger, clear Rosy's mouth of mucus and debris. Tilt her head back, hold her mouth shut with one hand, place your mouth over her nose. Blow into her nose until you see her chest begin to expand. Release her muzzle and allow the air to escape. Repeat the procedure every five seconds, keeping in mind that Rosy has a small lung capacity relative to your own. Don't blow with too much pressure or her lungs may rupture!

Pressure Bandage

Profuse bleeding is handled by locating the source of the spurting blood and applying a snug bandage directly over the source to quell the hemorrhage. Tie or tape the bandage securely in place and keep Rosy quiet. Use your jacket or a blanket as a stretcher to carry her, and to prevent further damage, handle her minimally.

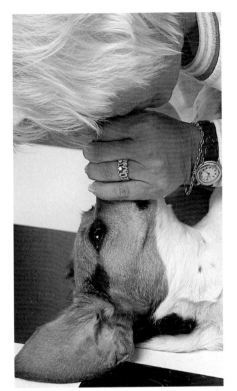

Hold the muzzle closed, place your mouth over the nose, and blow gently.

CPR

CPR stands for cardiopulmonary resuscitation and should be used if a dog's heart has stopped. One technique is to lay Rosy on her right side and with the heel of your hand press downward to compress her ribs and chest immediately behind her elbow. Press for a second then release. Continue this intermittent chest massage until her heart begins to beat on its own. If after a few minutes no heartbeat is noted, discontinue, wait a few seconds, and if no beating is felt, continue CPR.

Skin Lacerations

If Rosy steps on a broken bottle or a sharp tin can, or runs into a barbed wire fence, evaluate her injuries. If the wound is extensive or is bleeding profusely, immediately apply a pressure bandage and get her to a veterinarian. If the injury is only a minor scratch or tiny skin tear, clean with an antiseptic soap, apply antibiotic cream, and bandage if possible.

Pad Injuries

Lacerations or punctures involving only the pad leather may not require veterinary care, but should be bandaged to prevent further injury and contamination. After cleaning and applying antibiotic cream, place a snug but nonrestrictive bandage on the wounded foot and tape it in place. If you carry hunting boots for Rosy, put them on her.

Deep Punctures

When running in heavy cover, Rosy may impale herself on a sharp stick or nail. If the cause of the puncture isn't known, watch for bleeding, and apply a pressure bandage if needed. If a stick has broken off and remains in her flesh, leave it alone. Carry her to your car, keep her quiet, and transport her to a veterinarian. If you attempt to remove the stick, you might cause increased hemorrhage or you could leave a tiny piece of the stick lodged deep in the tissues where it is difficult to locate.

An immediate visit to Rosy's veterinarian is indicated in all cases of deep punctures to determine whether or not the wound has foreign material trapped within it. Always ask the veterinarian about tetanus antitoxin.

Fractures

Broken bones are another cause for alarm, but they require careful emergency treatment. If a leg is in a strange position, avoid handling it.

In case of any fracture, first evaluate shock and control hemorrhage. Then transport Rosy to the veterinarian as quickly as possible. Generally, no emergency splinting techniques should be used. Carry her on a board or makeshift stretcher if possible, and minimize movement of the fractured extremity.

Ear Wounds

Running hard in brush may result in an earflap laceration. When such a wound occurs, bleeding may be profuse and will be worsened by constant head shaking. Steady Rosy and bandage the torn ear snugly to the side of her head with gauze. Wrap the gauze with tape, overlapping the bandage and extending the tape onto the hair of her cheek. Ear wounds are less serious than other wounds, but bandaging a torn ear will save blood spatters on clothing

A deep pad wound should be bandaged for a few days.

and upholstery while on the trip to the veterinarian.

Nosebleeds

Determine the cause of a nosebleed first. If caused by light trauma, the hemorrhagic crisis usually is self-limiting if Rosy is kept quiet for half an hour. If more copious bleeding is seen, apply cold packs to her muzzle for several minutes and keep her quiet for half an hour after the bleeding stops.

If the bleeding isn't thought to be caused by trauma, keep her quiet and call your veterinarian. Such cases usually are associated with foreign objects like foxtails or cheat grass seeds in the nasal cavity.

Eartip wounds should be bandaged to the head.

Tourniquet

A tourniquet is the last resort for hemorrhage control and should be used only when there is no other way to stop bleeding. Use the rubber tube from your kit or fashion a tourniquet from a strip of gauze, a shoelace, a necktie, or any similar fabric item. When properly placed, a tourniquet slows the flow of arterial blood from the heart to the injured body part. If hemorrhage from Rosy's foot wound can't be stopped with pressure, place a tourniquet just above her ankle. If the wound is located on the trunk of the body, the head, or upper leg, a tourniquet can't be employed and a pressure bandage or finger pressure should be used to stop the hemorrhage.

When a tourniquet is used, tighten it only enough to stop the hemorrhage and release it for a few seconds every 15 minutes.

Poisoning

Poisoning presents a crisis and, if you suspect poisoning because of unexplained vomiting, weakness, or shock, keep Rosy quiet, take her vital signs, then make haste to the veterinary clinic. If you can locate some of the poisonous product or a label from the container, take it with you.

If the label instructs you to induce vomiting, you can accomplish that by placing about a teaspoonful of salt on the back of Rosy's tongue. A tablespoonful of hydrogen peroxide

Beagle tug-o-war.

may be administered orally, which will also produce vomiting. Syrup of ipecac may be used, but it is frequently slow to work.

Chocolate Poisoning

If the chocolate consumption is discovered immediately, rush Rosy to the veterinarian or induce vomiting as described previously.

At 400 mg per ounce, baking chocolate has the highest alkaloid content and is the most likely to cause trouble. Dark chocolate, with an alkaloid content of 150 mg per ounce, and milk chocolate, with a content of 50 mg per ounce, are less toxic but more readily available. For a 20-pound (9-kg) Beagle, 10,000 mg of alkaloid, or the amount found in 25 ounces of baking chocolate, will cause death. Much less can cause signs of poisoning, such as nervousness, vomiting, diarrhea, and urinary incontinence.

Instead of inducing vomiting, you may give activated charcoal to absorb the toxin. The correct dosage is 0.45 to 1.8 grams per pound of body weight, orally, in 2 to 4 ounces of water. Repeat this dosage every two to four hours.

If you bake with chocolate, remember the Beagle's appetite and always put the chocolate out of reach.

Chapter Seventeen

To Breed or Not to Breed

The big questions on this subject are *when, how,* and *why* or *why not.*

Six Poor Reasons to Breed

1. She will make a better companion (hunting) dog if she has a litter. This myth is unfounded in fact.

2. She will get fat if she isn't bred once. This is a cop-out for poor nutritional planning. If you monitor your Beagle's activities and adjust her diet accordingly, she won't get fat.

3. I want my children to witness the *miracle of birth.* If education is your motive, rent or buy a properly narrated video of childbirth. Videos are also available that include the birth of animals, both domestic and wild. Some of those films are diagrammatically illustrated for teaching purposes.

4. Puppies are so cute. Puppies are an obligation and commitment. The world is swarming with dogs that once were cute puppies. Millions of these cute puppies end up in shelters and pounds, unwanted, unloved, waiting to die after their brief stay in cramped cages. Over five million innocent, potentially good pets, many of them purebreds, are euthanized annually. Others manage to avoid capture to survive as feral animals in the alleys of urban America. If they avoid being maimed or killed by traffic, they live by their wits, scavenge from dumpsters, and serve as a reservoir of disease for our pets.

5. I want a puppy exactly like my Beagle. Beagles are individuals, and no two are identical. The best you can hope for is a Beagle puppy with half its genes from your well-loved dam. You might find the other half of the puppy's genes are all wrong. It's better to leave Beagle breeding to experts who study genetics and are able to produce superior puppies from carefully selected gene pools.

6. I want to recoup my investment by breeding her one time. Often avarice is the motive for dog breeding, but costs and time spent in caring for a brood bitch, and raising and vaccinating puppies negate any projected profit. Beagle pups produced from pet-quality bitches will rarely rise above pet quality, and owners of breeding-quality males aren't likely to allow their dogs to be used in a backyard-breeding program.

Breeding Your Beagle

Only one legitimate reason exists to support breeding your Beagle. If her proven excellence in conformation or performance will improve the breed, by all means, plan carefully and breed your Beagle.

If you're seriously considering raising puppies, consider these factors first.

Why

• You have invested in a show- and breeding-quality Beagle, and she has proven her merits in the show ring or field.
• She is free of hereditary diseases.
• You've found a proven high-quality stud dog that will complement her minimal faults.
• You can afford the costs associated with breeding and raising puppies.
• You have adequate facilities for breeding and raising a litter.
• You have the time and are prepared to take proper care of a brood bitch and her litter.
• You have the necessary contacts to place all the puppies in good homes.

If you have all these factors covered, you certainly don't want to have your Beagle bitch spayed.

How

Study the estrous cycle of dogs and make notes about your Beagle's cycle, its various stages, its duration, and the attitude of your bitch while in each stage. Prepare your Beagle for at least six months before breeding her; be sure she is enjoying the finest nutrition, is up to date on all vaccinations, and is harboring no parasites.

Study her pedigree, and with the help of Beagle breeders, choose a stud dog that complements her. Pay particular attention to the stud if your bitch is a 13-inch variety. Generally, Beagles are free-whelping dogs, but large puppies in a small bitch may cause the need for a cesarean section. Many small males sire larger puppies.

Study whelping procedures, dewclaw amputation, monitoring pups' weight, weaning, vaccinating, and finding good homes for all. Many books are available to assist you in Beagle breeding, such as *The Complete Book of Dog Breeding* by this author, published by Barron's Educational Series.

When

If you decide to breed your Beagle, wait until she is two years old and her veterinary examination has proven her to be free of hereditary diseases.

Brood Bitch Care

By five or six years of age, after your Beagle bitch has made her contribution to the gene pool, she should be retired. If breeding, pregnancy, or

This old-timer is still bright and alert, if a little gray.

whelping complications occurred, earlier retirement is prudent.

Female canines' reproductive lives end earlier than males, and by six years of age, a Beagle dam usually has passed her productive peak. After that age, reproductive problems and health risks are likely to increase with each passing year.

Retire your brood bitch before serious maladies begin to show up. Spay operations in older females are somewhat more difficult to perform, and there are slightly higher risks involved than in young animals, but those risks are minor compared to the risks of pyometra, tumors, and mammary cancer.

Ovariohysterectomy is the best insurance policy you can buy for your retired female Beagle.

Spaying

Spaying your female Beagle isn't just an arbitrary birth-control program. The surgery is a procedure wherein both ovaries and the uterus are removed (ovariohysterectomy); it is performed to extend her life by preventing several serious diseases. The operation is done under general anesthetic and minimal hospitalization time is required. She should be acting and eating normally within a few days.

Benefits of Spaying
• She no longer has three-week heat cycles twice a year.
• She can't become pregnant.
• If done early, prior to heat cycles, breast cancer rarely develops.

- It precludes the development of hormone-related conditions, such as pyometra and endometritis.
- It doesn't change her personality, ambition, trainability, growth, or development rate.

Castration or Vasectomy

Castration or neutering a male Beagle means the surgical removal of both testicles. Recovery should be uneventful and rapid, and after a few days he will be ready to tackle the world.

Vasectomy is quite a different procedure, in which the surgeon surgically transects and ties the vas deferens. These tubes are the channels through which the sperm travel. Vasectomy renders Sam sterile, but it doesn't alter his desire or ability to copulate. He still gets excited whenever a bitch in heat is nearby, and still runs off to find girlfriends at every opportunity.

Benefits
- Aggressiveness reduction is a benefit in some dogs, but Sam is the most even-tempered Beagle around.
- Testicular tumors, prostatitis, and prostatic cancer are averted by castration.
- Castration curbs the desire to wander in search of females in heat, and probably is the most common reason for the operation.
- Castration or neutering helps prevent the birth of unwanted puppies.

Reasons for Not Sterilizing

If your Beagle is purchased for showing or for AKC field trials, he or she shouldn't be sterilized until after the ring or field career is finished.

When to Spay or Castrate

Historically, female pets are spayed at five to six months of age because, if done before the first heat, the threat of breast cancer is eliminated.

Male pets usually are castrated at about 8 to 12 months, but this timing has also been challenged.

Spaying and neutering can be done much younger, and recent observations show earlier surgery to be safe, effective, and without personality problems. Recently, pets in shelters have been sterilized as early as 8 to 12 weeks of age with few, if any, problems. This has led to changes in the opinions of some breeders and ethologists (behavioral scientists) that may favor more early sterilization.

Is this new trend advisable? It's probably too soon to be sure. Thus far, experience and research indicate little or no negative impact on either physical development or personality, and the practice has brought about less euthanasia in American shelters and pounds.

Chapter Eighteen

Gone But Not Forgotten

Euthanasia

There are many reasons for giving your old friend a painless departure from the world. All are associated with a single factor; life has become a painful, confusing burden. It's best to call Rosy's veterinarian ahead of time and possibly take her to the hospital before regular office hours, so there will be no wait.

Administration of the lethal injection should always be done without anxiety. Her veterinarian will handle her gently and calmly, speaking to Rosy in comforting tones. The injection will be prepared in advance, so there will be no syringe being filled in her presence to alarm her. Sometimes, an assistant will steady the dog as the clinician makes a quick venipuncture. The lethal fluid is rapidly injected, and death follows instantly and painlessly.

Why Not Euthanize

There are hundreds of inappropriate reasons for putting a dog to sleep. Veterinarians have heard them all.

• If you haven't taken the time to train Rosy and teach her good manners, that's not her fault and isn't a legitimate excuse for euthanasia.
• If you suddenly find that her feeding and care are more trouble than she's worth, that's a human problem for you to deal with, not an excuse for ending a companion's life.
• She's ill or has been injured, and surgery, medication, and aftercare are more expense than you can afford. Have you explored every avenue available to you for financial help? Rescue organizations, no-kill animal aid institutions, and others may provide veterinary care.
• You're moving away and your new residence doesn't allow pets. Today, rescue associations and foster homes save many of these pets. Contact your local pound, shelter, or breed club for advice. Veterinarians often can put you in touch with no-kill facilities. Give Rosy another chance!

Reasons Supporting Euthanasia

Rosy is an old dog. She doesn't hear well, sleeps a lot, and her coat looks rather bedraggled. Her vision is failing, causing her to bump into objects at night. It's been months since she ran, barked, or bayed. Old joints hurt and she moves slowly and deliberately. Lately she's been leaving a damp spot on her rug where she's lain, and getting up seems to be an increasing chore. She's always been the cleanest dog alive, but recently she has accidents, then acts bewildered and ashamed.

You know Rosy isn't comfortable; it's time to give her up, but she's been such a wonderful dog you just can't bear the thought of taking this step. Maybe she'll not wake up in the morning. Wouldn't it be convenient if Rosy just went to sleep one night and didn't awaken? Unfortunately, that event is rare.

Her pleading, sad brown eyes look dimly for some comfort and relief from her pain. You reach for the aspirin and a bite of cheese to wrap it in and you know there isn't anything more you can do.

Finally, one day Rosy can't get to her feet. You carry her outside, but her rubbery legs won't support her and she falls, lying in a dejected heap. Suddenly, you know it's past time to give her the relief she's begged for the past weeks.

Euthanasia is the final act of love and kindness we can give our loyal Beagle. When a trusted veterinarian administers the lethal injection, Rosy will suffer no fear or apprehension. Stay with your old Beagle if you can; she'll appreciate it. Being beside her will tell her you haven't abandoned her, and your presence will reassure her.

When Rosy Is Gone

Rosy will never be forgotten, but don't waste your life with perpetual grieving and despair. She brought you happiness. Remember her, but don't bury yourself in her grave!

When you're ready for another dog, don't search for Rosy's clone. Dogs are individuals with different personalities, and there isn't another Beagle in the world just like Rosy. Maybe another pup from the same kennel, one that is closely related to her can be found, but she will never take Rosy's place.

Often it's best to seek a new Beagle that is quite different in appearance, a male instead of a female, or a smaller or larger one. Don't put undue pressure on the new Beagle; don't expect her or him to live up to Rosy's perfection.

Support Groups

Rosy's veterinarian can provide information about support groups. You will grieve your loss and you'll miss your old Beagle more than you think. Comfort yourself by attending group support meetings; if none is available, start a group. It's natural to lament the passing of a good friend, and sharing your loss with others makes the process easier.

You know that you shared your life with the best dog you ever met. Tomorrow will bring new adventures, a new relationship, a new Beagle.

Glossary

agility trial: Timed sporting event in which dogs must master a group of obstacles laid out on a course.

alpha dog: Leader of the pack; chief dog.

anthropomorphize: To attribute human characteristics to an animal.

aptitude: Natural ability or talent; general suitability.

associative learning: Method of teaching a dog by linking an act to a reward.

backyard breeder: Amateur or hobby producer of dogs, not necessarily interested in improving the breed.

beaglers: Individuals who are interested in Beagle activities.

beagling: Any activity involving exhibition of or interest in Beagles.

biddable: Cooperative dog, willing to obey handler.

bite: Position of dog's incisor teeth when mouth is closed.

body language: Physical attitude of a dog that tells handler what action dog is considering.

bond: Invisible reciprocal attachment between a dog and its master.

breeding quality: Possessing few, if any, faults and considered a candidate for propagation of the breed.

bumper: Stuffed canvas retrieving toy that resembles a boat fender.

canine cognitive dysfunction: Memory loss caused by old age.

Canis familiaris: Genus and species of domestic dog.

carnivore: Animal that subsists primarily on animal flesh.

champion: Dog that has competed in AKC shows or trials and earned sufficient points to be awarded Champion title.

CHD: Canine Hip Dysplasia; a hereditary deformity of femur and pelvis.

check cord or check line: Long, lightweight line attached to dog's collar to enable handler to control dog from a distance.

checked: Term used to describe a lost scent trail.

choke collar: Chain or nylon slip or check collar used for training.

cognitive ability: Capacity to understand or absorb knowledge.

conformation: Form and structure of dog compared to breed standard.

congenital disease: Deformity present at birth, not necessarily hereditary.

coprophagia: Feces eating.

crate training: Teaching dog to go to and stay in an enclosure.

cryptorchid: Dog with both testicles retained in abdominal cavity.

dead ring: On training collar, the ring through which the chain is dropped to form a noose.

dependence: Trust in and reliance of a dog on its handler.

direct negative reinforcement: Physical correction of a dog using a personal disciplinary measure such as scolding or hitting.

discipline: 1. Training in specific endeavor. 2. Chastisement or punishment. 3. Control.

dominance training: Activities for owners to use to establish themselves as dominant members of a dog's pack.

Elizabethan collar: A restrictive device placed on dog's neck to prevent licking parts of its body, usually fashioned from a stiff plastic sheet.

ethologists: Behavioral specialists.

feather: In Beagle body language, an excited twitching of the tail.

fecal exam: Microscopic examination of feces for evidence of parasite ova.

fetch: Game in which handler throws an article, which is recovered and returned by dog.

focus: Concentration of dog upon handler.

force: Physically causing dog to do something beyond its natural inclination. Restraint and dominance training are types of force. Force does not imply abuse.

gazehound: Hunting dogs that pursue their quarry by sight rather than scent.

gene pool: Collection of genes of all dogs in the breeding population.

habituation: Training by becoming accustomed or conditioned to a given incident or situation.

Harrier: A breed of dogs that are similar in appearance but slightly larger than Beagles and were developed in England to hunt hares.

heartworm: Bloodstream parasite of dogs, spread by mosquitoes.

hereditary: Genetically transmitted.

hyperactive: Displaying excessive activity with attention deficit.

imprinting: Rapid learning process that takes place early in the life of a social animal and establishes a behavior pattern.

innate: Inherent; natural; factors that are present from birth.

instinct: Natural or inherent aptitude.

intelligence: Ability to learn, understand, and solve problems through reasoning.

monorchid: Having one testicle retained in abdominal cavity.

mouthing: Normal action of a puppy investigating its environment by tasting.

negative reinforcement: Dissuading a dog from repeating an incorrect response to training by scolding or physically correcting the behavior.

neophobia: Fear of new things. Dominant characteristic of feral animals and undesirable in training prospects.

neoteny: Immature characteristics retained in adulthood.

nest etiquette: Manners governing young puppies' actions in presence of dam and siblings.

obedience: Discipline involving modification of many different behaviors through extensive training.

OFA: Orthopedic Foundation for Animals, the organization that analyzes and evaluates X rays for hereditary deformities.

olfactory sense: Ability to smell and differentiate odors.

olfactory system: Organs and tissues associated with smell.

overshot: Upper incisors that protrude over lowers.

pack: 1. Normal structure of a canine social community with a leader in charge. 2. A number of similar dogs in pursuit of a particular quarry.

pack mentality: Innate wolflike instinct of dog to be loyal to the pack leader, either canine or human.

pedigree: Genealogical chart of a dog showing a few generations of ancestors.

pet quality: Purebred dog with features that make it undesirable for conformation showing or breeding.

phenotype: Hereditary physical anatomical characteristics of an animal.

pheromones: Chemical substances secreted by animals that initiate a response from another animal. Usually not distinguishable by humans.

positive reinforcement: Any reward for proper performance.

progenitor: Ancestor or parent.

progeny: Offspring or descendents.

punishment: Physical negative reinforcement of a command.

puppy mill or puppy factory: Dog breeding establishment that places quantity above quality of puppies produced.

release: Command that returns the dog to its normal status.

remote reinforcement: Separated or distant tool used to assist in training; squirt bottle, long line, noise.

retracting lead: Long leash contained within a spring-loaded handle that can be drawn in quickly.

reward: Any recognized appreciation given to dog being trained.

scenthound: Hunting dog that follows quarry by its scent.

selective breeding: Scientific mating to encourage or produce specific characteristics in offspring.

show quality: Registered dogs having excellent conformation, color, and movement according to breed standard.

siblings: Brothers and sisters born to same litter.

snipy: Weak, pinched, or pointed muzzle.

socialization: Process of adapting to a human environment.

submissive or subservient attitude: Combination of postures taken by a puppy when meeting other dogs.

temperament: Personality; mental attitude or character of a dog.

tidbits: Physical rewards or food.

toilet area: Designated spot in the yard where a dog goes to defecate and urinate.

tongue: Giving voice or sound when on the trail of quarry.

trainability: Ability and desire to learn; propensity of a dog to focus on handler and accept direction.

training ring: Ring on training collar to which leash is snapped.

umbilical hernia: Congenital out-pouching of abdominal tissues resulting from lack of fusion of muscles.

undershot: Lower incisors protruding beyond uppers.

wait: Command used to tell dog that you will return shortly.

work-play balance: Essential part of any training that refers to the necessity to intermingle training with play.

worm check: Fecal examination to determine endoparasite infestation.

xenophobia: Attitude of a dog that exhibits fear or hate of strangers.

Useful Addresses and Literature

Organizations

American Boarding Kennel
  Association
4675 Galley Road, Suite 400-A
Colorado Springs, CO 80915

American Humane Association
9725 E. Hampton Avenue
Denver, CO 80231

American Kennel Club (AKC)
5580 Centerview Drive, Suite 200
Raleigh, NC 27606-3390

American Rabbit Hunting
  Association
Box 244
Hoskinston, KY 40844

American Veterinary Medical
  Association
930 N. Meacham Road
Schaumburg, IL 60173

BONE (Beagle Obedience Network
  Excellent)
Denise Nord
14605 34th Avenue #317
Plymouth, MN 55447

Canine Eye Registry Foundation
  (CERF)
South Campus Court, Building C
West Lafayette, IN 47907

The Delta Society
289 Perimeter Road East
Renton, WA 98055-1329

Heartland Federation of Beagle
  Clubs Inc.
304 Dickerson Lane
Falmouth, KY 41040

Institute for Genetic Disease
  Control (GDC)
P.O. Box 222
Davis, CA 95617

International Beagle Federation
54 Sun Valley Lane
Finleyville, PA 15332

Mid-Dixie Beagle Federation
459 Lester Road
Fayetteville, GA 30214

National Association of Dog
  Obedience Instructors
2286 E. Steele Road
St. Johns, MI 48879

National Beagle Club (NBC)
22265 Oatlands Road
Aldie, VA 22005

National Dog Registry (tattoo,
   microchip)
P.O. Box 116
Woodstock, NY 12498

National Research Council (NRC)
Nutritional Requirements of Dogs,
   Revised
1-800-624-6242

Northeastern Beagle Gundog
   Federation
423 E. Second Avenue
South Williamsport, PA 17701

Northern Association of Beagle
   Clubs
10414 Devil's Lake Highway
Addison, MI 49220

Owners Handlers Association of
   America
RD 1, Box 32
Urbana, IL 61801

Orthopedic Foundation for
   Animals (OFA)
2300 Nifong Blvd.
Columbia, MO 65201

Tattoo-A-Pet
Dept. 1625
Emmons Avenue
Brooklyn, NY 11235

Therapy Dogs International
91 Wiman Avenue
Staten Island, NY 10308

United Kennel Club (UKC)
100 E. Kilgore Rd
Kalamazoo, MI 49001-5592

United States Dog Agility Association
P.O. Box 850955
Richardson, TX 75085-0955

Magazines

AKC Gazette
260 Madison Avenue
New York, NY 10016

Beagle Fox Hound Magazine, The
10428 Morning Star Road
Bentonville, AR 72712

Better Beagling
P.O. Box 8142
Essex, VT 05451

Brace Beagling News
25130 – 75th Street
Paddock Lake, MI 53168

Dog Fancy
P.O. Box 53264
Boulder, CO 80322-3264

Dog World
29 N. Wacker Drive
Chicago, IL 60606

Front and Finish (Obedience
   Magazine)
P.O. Box 333
Galesburg, IL 61402

Hounds and Hunting
P.O. Box 372
Bradford, PA 16701

Off-Lead (Training Magazine)
P.O. Drawer A
Clark Mills, NY 13321

Purebred Dogs
AKC Gazette
260 Madison Avenue
New York, NY 10016

Rabbit Hunter, The
P.O. Box 557
Royston, GA 30662

Show Beagle Quarterly
P.O. Box 2340
Redlands, CA 92373

Small Pack Option, The
P.O. Box 569
Greene, NY 13778

On the Web

The Beagle Brigade
USDA APHIS
acherry@aphis.usda.gov

Books for Additional Reading

Alderton, David. *Dogs.* New York: DK Publishing Co., 1993.

American Kennel Club. *The Complete Dog Book.* New York: MacMillan Publishing Co., 1992.

Bennett, Bill. *The Care, Training and Hunting of the Beagle.* New York: Doral Publishing Co., 1995.

Brace, Andrew. *Beagles Today.* New York: MacMillan Publishing Co., 1997.

Bryson, Sandy. *Search and Rescue Dog Training.* Pacific Grove, CA: Boxwood Press, 1976.

Clark, Ross D. and Stainer, Joan R. *Medical and Genetic Aspects of Purebred Dogs.* Fairway, KS and St. Simons Island, GA: Forum Publications, Inc., 1994.

Coren, Stanley. *The Intelligence of Dogs.* New York: The Free Press, Division of MacMillan, Inc., 1994.

Davis, Henry P. *The Modern Dog Encyclopedia.* Harrisburg, PA: The Stackpole Co., 1958.

Lorenz, Michael D. and Cornelius, Larry M. *Small Animal Diagnosis.* Phildadelphia, PA: J.B. Lippincott Company, 1993.

Pearsall, Milo and Verbruggen, Hugo. *Scent.* Loveland CO: Alpine Publications, Inc., 1982.

Musladin, Musladin, and Lueke. *A Dog for All Seasons.* New York: Howell Book House, 1990.

Rice, Dan F. *The Complete Book of Dog Breeding.* Hauppauge, NY: Barron's Educational Series, Inc., 1997.

Saunders, Blanche. *Complete Book of Dog Obedience.* New York: Howell Book House, 1969.

Simmons-Moake, Jane. *Agility Training.* New York: Howell Book House, 1991.

Syrotuck, William G. *Scent and the Scenting Dog.* Canastota, NY: Arner Publications, Inc., 1972.

Waters, B. *Fetch and Carry.* Printed in 1895 by B. Waters.

Index